FOSSIL THIEF

A Henrietta Ballantine Adventure

SHARON LYON

FOSSIL WOMAN SERIES BOOK 2

∞

For Logan

CHAPTER 1

Organ music blared from the sanctuary, echoing across the narthex and rattling the door behind which I hid.

"Henrietta, your veil is crooked." Delilah's brow furrowed as she reached up and adjusted the combs digging into my head.

"Ouch. I can't see a thing through all this netting," I said. "And this dress is scratchy." I pulled on the skirt of my wedding gown.

Delilah, my best friend since we were thrown together as freshmen roommates at the College of William & Mary, glared at me. Her auburn hair escaped from her topknot, forming a cascade of curls around her face. Although she wore the turquoise bridesmaid dress my mother selected, she paired it with a clunky silver peace sign necklace, not being able to resist a political statement.

"Stop complaining," she said. "You look great. Are you ready?"

Two weeks ago I marched down the center aisle at the university field house, crossed a stage, and accepted the diploma for my PhD. After four long years of fieldwork, classes, research, data analysis, writing, revising, presenting, and defending, I was now Dr. Henrietta Ballantine.

Today, moments away from walking down another aisle, my heart stampeded in my chest. I was a hundred times more nervous.

"I'm as ready as I'll ever be," I said, inhaling deeply. Delilah jammed the bridal bouquet into my shaking hands. My dad rested on a chair in a corner, looking distinguished in his rented tuxedo. He was determined to walk without his cane, a remnant of a lab accident years before. A paleontologist at the Smithsonian National Museum of Natural History, my dad had always been my biggest supporter. He guided my education, cheered my successes, and helped me navigate my mother's moods.

With a suppressed groan, he rose from the chair, straightened his jacket, and crooked his arm toward me. "You look beautiful, honey," he said. "Here we go."

Delilah stepped ahead of us, pushed open the door, and crossed to the back of the nave. Her appearance at the last pew cued the organist to switch music. Holding her bouquet of roses and baby's breath, she paraded inside. Then my dad pulled me along like a moon in his orbit, the congregation rising. As sixty pairs of eyes swiveled to stare at me, all my nerve endings fired. I hated being the center of attention. Tears unwittingly sprung into my eyes. I marched toward the front, the blare of the bridal march jarring my brain.

Sunlight blazed through the stained-glass windows like a celestial blessing. Delilah's husband, Kelvin, now an ordained minister, stood at the altar in his vestments. His long hair and bushy beard made him appear as Jesus himself. To my right, filling my vision, was my soon-to-be-husband, Frank. After years of a mostly long-distance relationship, we would now be spending every day together. I imagined our lives would be magical from here on. If only this ceremony would proceed at the speed of light.

Flanked by his two brothers, Frank smiled his crooked half grin, watching me approach. Tall, handsome, a fellow geologist, he winked at me as I reached his side.

The music ceased. "Who gives this woman to be married to this man?" Kelvin asked, as if I were chattel.

"I do," my dad responded. He handed me over with a kiss and a handshake.

A glance behind me revealed my well-coiffed mother, relief on her face, dabbing her eyes with a tissue. Next to her, my dear Aunt Esther smiled brightly.

"Dearly Beloved . . ." began Kelvin.

Before I knew it, Frank was kissing me and I was now Mrs. Frank Bailey. Or was I Dr. Henrietta Bailey? Or Dr. Henrietta Ballantine-Bailey? I was now both a wife and an expert in African Ice Age plants, my dissertation topic. Surely with those qualifications, my future would burn as bright as a supernova.

White silk bows and damask tablecloths dressed the folding tables in the church basement. A three-tiered cake topped with plastic bride and groom figurines tottered next to the buffet. Trays overflowed with tea sandwiches, deviled eggs, and pigs in a blanket while jiggling gelatin molds congealed in multiple colors not found in nature. The church ladies catering our wedding reception festivities lurked in the kitchen like Cold War spies. My mother circulated and glanced at her watch, having scheduled this soiree down to the minute.

Delilah and Aunt Esther chatted in a corner. I sidled up next to Delilah and eavesdropped. She was on a roll. "Esther, you must know this war is a tragedy," she said. "Kelvin and I are determined to make the politicians listen. Our voices must be heard."

Aunt Esther seemed mesmerized by Delilah's peace sign necklace. "But what about communism?" she asked in her southern drawl. "Shouldn't we try to stop it?"

"Not by spilling American blood," Delilah answered. "The French were in Vietnam for years. What did that accomplish?"

I interrupted her. "It's good to see you haven't lost your debating skills after four years." She and I had been members of a debating society, the Philomatheans, at William & Mary.

"Just think of the debates the Philomatheans could have now about this war," Delilah replied. "Who'd want to take the pro argument, I wonder? I can't imagine anyone on a college campus arguing that side."

My mother swooshed toward us in drapes of mauve and sparkles of sequins. She heard Delilah's last comment and halted next to her.

"Oh, for heaven's sake, Delilah, must you talk about the war *today*?" she asked, her brow creasing.

"Today and every day, Mrs. B," she replied. "It's my duty as a free American."

My mother waved a hand across her face and looked at her watch. "Henrietta, it's time for you and Frank to cut the cake."

Heaven forbid we not follow the schedule.

"All right," I said. "I'll go grab him."

Frank sat at a table across the room with his brothers. A flask disappeared into his oldest brother's pocket as I approached.

"Sorry to pull you away from the subterfuge," I said, tilting my head toward the hidden flask. "But Mother says it's time to cut the cake."

He beamed at me. "Your wish is my command, wife," he said as his brothers snickered. He got up and reached for my hand, and we walked across the floor toward the tiered confection.

The crowd quieted as we posed behind the cake. Flashbulbs blazed. We cut into the bottom layer and fed each other a bite. I chewed. The frosting's distinct taste and texture rolled around on my tongue.

Frank leaned over and whispered in my ear. "Is this frosting made of coconut?"

I almost choked, holding back a laugh. "Yes, your favorite, right?" I whispered, conspiratorially.

When Frank first met my mother, she had baked a coconut cake for dessert, and trying to make a good impression, he told her it was his favorite. The truth was, Frank hated coconut.

"I guess I'll be eating coconut until death do us part," he said.

I nodded. "Afraid so."

The church ladies stepped in, shoving us aside to slice the bottom two layers of the cake. Pieces disappeared like the biblical loaves and fishes.

The noise level rose as the Bailey's sugar-saturated progeny began to run amok. Frank's brothers had reproduced prolifically in the past four years, and he was now an uncle to five little boys. And now I was—*yikes*—an aunt.

Someone substituted whatever music my mother had selected on the phonograph for an LP by the Beach Boys and cranked up the volume to "Barbara Ann."

"Auntie Henrietta! Watch me dance!" one of the kids yelled at me from across the room—was it Jeffrey? I had yet to tell them apart.

He jumped around and grabbed his brothers, or cousins, or whoever they were, and mayhem ensued. Frank's brothers joined in, and an odd spectacle resulted: twisting, gyrating limbs interspersed with hooting, leaping children. Delilah dragged Kelvin into the mix, and they executed a rendition of the dance known as the Jerk. Either that or they were having some kind of coordinated seizure.

From the corner of my eye, I saw my mother, her eyes squinted and her mouth agape. Like a fox to its den, she retreated to the safety of the church kitchen.

Frank draped his arm around my shoulders. "Isn't this great?" he asked, nodding toward his dancing brethren. A wide smile spread across his face as he bopped along with the music. "My nephews are in the groove. What a hoot. I can't wait to be a dad."

My stomach fell like a meteor. All the air disappeared from my lungs. I could not help it—I pulled away from him, wide-eyed. "Frank, I said *someday*. Maybe someday we'd have a child. Not now. Not *soon*."

He continued to watch the dancers, distracted. "Oh yeah, I know, I know." Pulled by some invisible force I did not understand, he left my side and joined the whirling mob.

I stood and watched them, mesmerized, like analyzing data from a spectrograph. What was the attraction of children? Granted, my childhood had been somewhat abnormal, being homeschooled and studying at the Smithsonian. I had been a loner. Then I met and fell in love with Frank. Now we were a partnership, a complete whole.

Why would I want to upset that balance? Deep inside I also knew this truth—at that moment, certainly, more than being a mother, I wanted one thing. And that was to continue my work as a paleontologist. As happy as I was to finally marry Frank—and he had waited four years for me to finish graduate school—I was not going to let anything stand in my way. Motherhood would certainly do that. Like a huge, enormous, vast, impenetrable stone wall.

My Aunt Esther appeared at my side, joining me in watching the rabble. "Congratulations, my dear. Although I guess one no longer is supposed to say 'congratulations' to the bride. It gives the idea that she succeeded in catching a husband."

I leaned over and hugged her. "Thank you. I wish Uncle Al could've been here."

"Yes, he would've loved to see you happy and married," she said, her soft voice catching and her eyes a little teary. "I like to think he's looking down on us as we speak."

Standing together, arm in arm, we watched the writhing mob of boys and men.

The white paper streamers decorating our brand-new Ford Country Squire station wagon fluttered in the breeze as we rushed from the church, dodging the rain of rice tossed at us by our guests. I ducked my head and laughed as Frank opened the passenger door, helping me shove in the yards of tulle composing my dress. He slammed the door and ran to the driver's side. With his head down as more rice pummeled him, he leaped behind the wheel. I stuck my hand out the window to wave goodbye as we pulled out of the parking lot. Tin cans tied to our bumper raised a racket as we drove down Columbia Pike.

"I've got to get rid of those cans," Frank said, pulling into a residential side street. "We can't drive into the District dragging them behind us." He jammed the car into park and, with some imaginative cursing, managed to extract the offending noisemakers. He tossed them into the back seat.

"All right, let's get this honeymoon started, Mrs. Bailey," he said with a grin.

"Ready when you are, husband," I said, winking at him.

We drove into Rosslyn and crossed the Potomac River by way of the Key Bridge. Far below us, tumbling water rushed to bypass rocky islands of metabasalt, continuing on its journey to the Chesapeake Bay. Arriving in Georgetown, we followed Wisconsin Avenue to a five-story pink brick building and pulled under the portico. The Georgetown Inn was the most expensive hotel in the city at twenty-two dollars a night.

"It was nice of your parents to give us a two-night stay here as a wedding gift," I said. "I wonder if we'll see any celebrities?"

Frank lifted one eyebrow at me. "I couldn't care less," he said.

Suffice it to say, since we had not seen each other without chaperones for over a month, once we reached our room we wasted no time in getting rid of all that stupid netting and formal wear. Afterward, as the sun set over the river and the traffic noises quieted outside, I snuggled next to Frank under the luxurious satin sheets and allowed my blissful heart to lull me into a cavern of sleep.

CHAPTER 2

Back at my parents' house two days later, I glanced around my childhood bedroom, memories flitting in and out of my mind like gossamer threads. My dormer window, through which I had stared at the heavens and memorized the constellations, stood open to let in fresh air. My bookcase, now empty, had housed my first fledgling fossil collection. The twin bed where I spent hours indulging my love of reading seemed tiny and forlorn.

For most of my childhood, I had been unseen. Homeschooled with minimal contact with anyone my age. My father had characterized me as "shy." I was "an absolute stick," according to my mother. My salvation had been the hours I spent in the Smithsonian National Museum, thanks to my dad's position. Every Friday had been my "museum study day," and I had taken advantage of my access to the behind-the-scenes repository of fossils. Weekly discussions with the scientists who worked there had bolstered my ability to ask the right questions and to seek answers. Then, while attending college and digging at geological sites across the country, I continued to fulfill my passion for paleontology. I had even traveled to Africa and dug for early human remains with the Leakey team. Today, that all seemed a million years ago.

I felt weatherworn, having survived the grind of graduate school. I was ready for the next challenge, arm in arm with Frank. Pushing aside memories of the reticent person who had lived here, I grabbed the last box.

"How many more boxes do you have?" my dad called out.

"Just one more. I want to put my sediment samples from Olduvai Gorge on top of the rest."

I turned my back on my ghosts and left the barren room.

Crates containing my meticulously packed fossil collection now rested under the attic eaves. Miocene shark teeth, pelecypods, and gastropods from Williamsburg. Petrified Carboniferous tree stumps and fern impressions from coal country. Utah's Cambrian trilobites. Wyoming's Green River fish.

"I guess all these boxes would be too bulky to fit in your station wagon," my dad said, a rueful smile crossing his face.

"Yeah, considerably." I returned his grin. "And we need to leave all the new china and crystal that Mother insisted I register for. None of that's going to fit either."

"Don't worry about all that. I'll get Frank to help me carry it to the basement once he gets back from seeing his parents off. I know they wanted to get an early start back to New Jersey," he said, glancing at his wristwatch.

"Rocks in the attic and fine china in the cellar," I said. "A girl's gotta have priorities."

My dad tapped on the boxes. "You can always come back and pick these up. Morgantown isn't that far away. Although I know you'll want to spend your weekends in the field this summer."

"Yes, Frank and I have our fieldwork planned out," I said. "He's going to teach me the local stratigraphy. And I'm anxious to start learning more about the fossil plants that lived in the Pennsylvanian coal swamps. Just think about the diversity in those ancient forests."

My dad nodded. "Not to mention the giant amphibians and early reptiles," he said, always the vertebrate paleontologist. He brushed some dust off the front of his shirt. "It'll be good to have that field experience under your belt before you start teaching your Historical Geology class in the fall."

Frank had kept his promise to me—once I finished graduate school, he would stop working in the coal industry, an environment-destroying business I abhorred. Instead, he had searched for a position working in petroleum. Surely more ecologically friendly than coal, I thought, with hope in my heart. He had received a verbal offer from a small firm, Monroe Petroleum. The company was headquartered in North Dakota, and they had flown him out there for an interview. Monroe was opening an exploration office in Morgantown, West Virginia, and Frank, with his Appalachian stratigraphy experience, had been a perfect fit. We were awaiting the written offer, which he had requested to be sent to my parents' mailbox.

The puzzle pieces had shifted into place for me as well. I would start as an instructor at the university in Morgantown. Although part-time at first, I hoped the position would expand into a professorship. I was ready to prove my worth.

"I can't wait to teach that class," I said to my dad. "Once I get established, I'll be able to do research with students. We could even partner with some of the scientists at the museum. I think Dr. Brown is interested in ferns and lycopods. And, who knows? Maybe a student will want to work on fossil fish."

Fossil fish were my dad's specialty. "I'm always ready for collaboration," he said, smiling at me.

My joy beamed across my face as I handed him the last box. He shoved it into place, more dust sprinkling down from the eave above. I picked up a marker and wrote "Olduvai Gorge samples" on the box.

The past was now packed away, literally. My future awaited.

———

That afternoon, I meandered outside to the backyard. A few cumulus clouds wafted in the unstable air overhead. Sparrows chirped despondently in the heat, and I wiped sweat from my forehead. I studied the back of my parents' clapboard house. The windows appeared newly washed, and the trim shined with fresh paint. I was about to sit on my old swing, still hanging under the chokecherry trees, when I heard a voice.

"Henrietta! Hello!"

My next-door neighbor, Lana Sawyer, hailed me from her patio. I turned my head and gaped at her, surprised she even remembered my name. Lana had been my nemesis growing up. She and her toadies had either teased or ignored me throughout my childhood. It had not helped that she was pretty.

Today, however, as she walked over to the chain-link fence, I noticed that her hair, pulled back in a low ponytail, looked rather lackluster, and dark circles rimmed her eyes. Also, she was pregnant. A toddler played behind her on the concrete slab from where she used to torment me.

"Hello, Lana. Is that your little boy?" I asked, walking over to the fence.

"Yes, and my daughter is inside with Mom," she said. She patted her tummy. "And number three is due in October."

"Congratulations."

"Thanks. I married Robby Winterbottom. Do you remember him?" she asked, pushing a stray hair out of her face.

"No."

She squinted into the sun. "No, you probably wouldn't. You never seemed concerned with all the boy-girl drama."

"I was homeschooled, remember? I didn't know many people."

"Yeah, I always wondered about that," she said. "You know, I always envied you, Henrietta."

My heart skipped a beat. "What? You envied *me*?"

"Yeah. You were always so smart. Remember when you told our Sunday school teacher about evolution? And how Noah's ark couldn't be true? I thought she'd blow a gasket!"

I smiled at the memory. "Oh yes, I definitely remember that. She strongly suggested I not return until I'd changed my view. So I never returned."

She snorted a laugh. "That figures. By the way, congratulations to you! I heard you just got married. My mom hears all the gossip."

"Thanks. We're moving in a day or two to West Virginia," I said.

Lana's son called over. "Mommy! I'm hungry!"

She heaved a sigh and glanced behind her. "Got to go. Nap time. Good luck in West Virginia. And congrats again." With a weary smile, she gave a small wave and turned back toward her son. As I watched her shuffle away, I mused over her words.

Lana Sawyer had envied me? The earth's magnetic poles must have reversed polarity. It sure was a topsy-turvy world. In any case, my compass now pointed northwest, toward the Allegheny Plateau.

But I was about to learn that destiny is a devil with a mind of its own.

My mother called to me from the living room as she sorted through a stack of envelopes in her hands. "Henrietta, that letter arrived in the mail, for Frank. The one you've been waiting for. From the oil company."

"Thanks, Mother," I replied, the back door swinging as I entered the kitchen. We met halfway, in the dining room, and she handed the letter to me. I noticed a slight slump in her shoulders as she suppressed a yawn. All those wedding details must have worn her down.

"'Dr. Frank Bailey,'" I read from the envelope. "I guess I shouldn't open it."

My mother's eyes opened wide. "Of course not," she said in a sharp voice. "It's illegal to open someone else's mail."

"Even your husband's?"

"Especially your husband's," she said, the lines creasing at the edges of her mouth. "You don't want to start your marriage like that."

Like what? I did not ask.

Frank saved me from further discussion as he came through the front door, letting it bang closed behind him. My mother flinched at the sound.

She turned toward him. "Did your family get on the road?" she asked.

"Yes, and they said to thank you again for your hospitality," Frank said with a careful smile. "They had a wonderful time."

"Well, it was lovely to *finally* meet them," she said, with emphasis on the "finally."

Jeez.

I waved the letter in front of Frank. "Here it is!" I said. "It just came in the mail. Your formal offer from Monroe Petroleum."

He crossed the living room in two steps, reached for the letter, and held it up in front of his eyes as if to read it through the envelope with X-ray vision. "Okay, here goes." He took a deep breath. "Let's see what salary they're offering me."

My mother had enough sense to disappear into the kitchen.

Frank tore open the envelope. Plunking himself down on one of the stiff dining room chairs, he spread the letter on the table, smoothing out the folds as if it were a priceless heirloom. He began to read. The anticipation on his face faded, the edges of his mouth turning down. His brow crinkled as his eyes traveled down the page.

"What's wrong?" I asked. "Isn't the salary what you thought it would be?"

He pursed his lips and swallowed. "It's not that."

"What is it, then?" I asked, lowering myself onto the chair next to him. "Tell me."

"They've offered me a position as a petroleum geologist."

I nodded in his direction. "Yes, you knew that, right?"

"But it isn't in Morgantown."

"Oh. Is it in a town nearby?" I asked. "Somewhere else in West Virginia, so I can commute to the university?"

He looked up from the letter, his eyes seeking mine. "Henrietta, they've decided not to open the office in West Virginia," he said. "The job is in Dickerson. North Dakota."

As my stomach hardened into a hard knot, Frank pulled me outside, away from my mother's eavesdropping presence in the kitchen. I climbed down the front porch steps in a daze. Virginia's summer humidity made my skin feel instantly clammy. Children giggled from a yard across the street, oblivious to my distress. We crossed the front yard and turned along the sidewalk, leaving the house behind us.

"North Dakota?" I moaned. My feet pounded the concrete, like an angry metronome with a staccato cadence. Frank walked next to me, allowing me to vent. "What about my job at the university? What the heck am I supposed to do in North Dakota?"

"I'm sorry, Henrietta. I'm not sure," he said, reaching down and grabbing my hand. "But I've already given notice at National Bitumen. It's not like we have a choice."

I slowed my pace, scuffing along, a half step behind Frank, in silence for several blocks as I let the reality of our new situation infiltrate my brain. In my mind's eye, I envisioned my teaching position evaporating into the air like a mud puddle on a warm day. Tears threatened at the corners of my eyes.

Finally, we stopped at a crosswalk.

My lip quivered. "I know, you're right—we don't have a choice. My salary for teaching part-time wouldn't even cover the rent on an apartment in Morgantown."

"No, we can't move to West Virginia if I don't have a job there," Frank said.

"But it's okay for me to move to North Dakota without one?" I whined, afraid to look up and show my salt-rimmed eyes.

He looked down at me. "There is good news. The letter said the company has set up housing for us if we want it. A furnished house in a nearby town. And the rent is affordable."

"So we wouldn't be living in Dickerson?" I asked.

"No, the house is in a town called Mammoth. I've never been there." He squeezed my hand. "We don't have to take the house if you don't want to. We can drive out there and look for a place to rent in Dickerson. But I've sunk a lot of my savings into our new car. And it might be easier to accept the house and not have to worry about finding a place. Or furnishing one."

I sniffled and swiped my sleeve across my face. Resignation began to settle into my chest. "You went to Dickerson for your interview. What's that town like?"

"It's a small town, a lot smaller than Arlington. Or even Williamsburg. They have a grocery store and a drugstore and a library. There might be a movie theater."

I raised my eyes to the sky, resenting the overhanging cotton candy clouds for their cheerful appearance. And what nerve did those sparrows have to twitter in the hedges?

"How about a college?" I asked.

"Oh, no, honey. Dickerson isn't that big. I think the closest university is way over on the Minnesota border. We'll be closer to Montana. To be honest, there's not much in that part of the state except for oil fields. And Indian reservations."

"I'll bet the winters are cold out there," I said with an imaginative shiver.

A greater understatement has yet to be uttered.

***

That evening, an uncomfortable hush surrounded us at my parents' dining table. Frank had called Monroe Petroleum, accepted the job offer, and told them we wanted the rental house. My throat raw and my heart heavy, I had written a letter to the chairman of the Geology Department in Morgantown, informing him I would not be able to teach in the fall. Even my mother's sumptuous pot roast, one of my favorites, failed to uplift my spirits.

My dad broke the silence. "You'll be going to a great place for fossil hunting, you know. You'll be at the edge of the badlands. Which is chock-full of dinosaur bones."

I nodded dully and stuffed a bite of potato in my mouth.

He persisted. "I just read an article about a new genus called *Deinonychus*. The name means 'terrible claw.' John Ostrom, at Yale, argues that this new dinosaur was agile and intelligent. Not the slow, dim-witted traits we associate with dinosaurs."

I swallowed the potato, which felt like a lump of lead in my throat. "I wonder how someone joins a dinosaur dig."

My dad shrugged. "Dinosaur digs are usually sponsored by universities. Unfortunately, the field season will be half over by the time you get there."

"Well, there's no university near our town anyway," I said, staring at my plate.

My dad was on a roll, blind to the tension in the room. "Dinosaurs are flashy, yes, but don't forget—the badlands' strata preserve other creatures as well. Cretaceous mammals occupied diverse niches among the dinosaurs. Although they were small, I'd argue that studying the evolution of mammals is just as important as discovering a new dinosaur species. If not more so."

With resignation on my face, I looked at my father, a staunch evolutionist. I appreciated him trying to keep up my spirits. "I agree," I said. "And they lived in ecosystems with the Mesozoic flora. Which I know something about."

"Yes, you do, Dr. Paleobotanist," he said with pride in his voice.

Frank turned to me. "Maybe we can hike around the badlands on our own on the weekends. And scout around for fossils."

"Maybe," I said.

My dad added, "If you do that, make sure you know who owns the land. You don't want to be shot by some rancher."

"Oh, for heaven's sake, Harry," my mom said. "I don't want to hear any talk about people getting shot. Henrietta, maybe you'll be able to find some kind of temporary job in Mammoth. Doing something safer than being shot at in the badlands."

"I'll try to figure out something work-wise once I get there," I added without much enthusiasm.

My mom rose from her chair. "You should be happy that Frank has such a good position. It seems to me that you should be celebrating his new job offer instead of moping around." She turned and disappeared into the kitchen.

I sat, stunned by her words. Perhaps I *was* being selfish.

She came back into the dining room with a cake displayed on a pedestal plate. "For dessert, I've made lemon poppyseed cake," she announced, setting the dessert in the middle of the table.

Nothing like sugar and white flour to solve the world's problems.

Later that night, lying in the bed in my parent's spare bedroom, surrounded by our packed suitcases, Frank whispered in my ear. "It will be all right, Henrietta. I'll make sure of it."

With those words, I trusted him with my whole heart. After all, I thought, swiveling my wedding band around my finger with my thumb, what choice did I have?

CHAPTER 3

"Wait, Henrietta," my mother called from the porch. "You forgot your cookbook." Holding the red *Betty Crocker's Picture Cook Book* in her hands, she stepped down and crossed to the driveway.

"Thanks, Mother," I said, taking it from her. She had given the book to me for my thirteenth birthday so I would know how to cook for my "future husband." Poor Frank. It had gathered dust in a kitchen cabinet since then.

My mother leaned over and hugged me in an awkward embrace. "Don't forget to write," she said.

"I will," I said, my mind elsewhere. I hugged my dad, walked around the car, and slid into the passenger seat next to Frank. Turning to look behind me into the back of the station wagon, I saw no space to shove the cookbook. Instead, I plunked it on the floor and set my feet on it.

With the Supremes crooning "You Can't Hurry Love," Frank backed out of the driveway. We waved goodbye and headed westward. The sun rose behind us, and a hot breeze blew through the open windows. I settled back into the seat, resigned to be moving to North Dakota and ready for a long drive.

"Thank goodness you didn't forget that cookbook," said Frank, crinkle lines forming around his eyes.

I leaned down and picked the binder up off the floor, flipping the pages across the metal rings. "Oh, yeah. Let me see. What am I going to cook for you first? How about 'Crispy Brown Hash, a favorite of Mrs. Paul Doherty of Evanston, Illinois'? Or 'Calf's Liver Supreme, a famous home recipe of Mrs. Ernst Halloway of California'?"

"Now you're just trying to make me nauseous," he said.

"What makes me nauseous is that these women have lost their first names," I said. "And their identity." I paused for a moment. "I've been thinking—would you care if I didn't change mine?"

Frank glanced over at me. "Your identity?" He grinned. "Are we going into Witness Protection for some reason I don't know about?"

I returned his smile. "No. Seriously, though. Would you mind if I didn't change my last name? Professionally anyway. I could still be called 'Mrs. Bailey' in social settings, but I'd use 'Dr. Ballantine' at work."

His smile faded. "Really? Does that mean you wouldn't legally change your name to Bailey?"

I exhaled. "No, I wouldn't. It isn't that I don't like the name Bailey," I hurried to reassure him. "It's just that my degrees say Ballantine. I think it would be confusing when I'm looking for a job."

"I think it might be more confusing if you use two names," he said, his mouth now set in a stubborn pucker. "I assume our kids will have my last name, right?"

Kids? Arg.

My heart thudded against my rib cage. "Sure. Of course."

"Babe, I guess if you want to keep your name, then I won't object. Just don't tell my mother. She'd pitch a fit."

"Oh, yeah. Ditto with mine," I said.

After a few hours, our car climbed in elevation as we abandoned the crystalline rocks of the Piedmont for the Precambrian metasediments of the Blue Ridge. That night, camping along Skyline Drive, we reminisced about our cross-country trek taken years earlier, when we first met as students, viewing some of these same rocks with younger eyes. As the earth spun on its rotational axis, the constellations marched across the celestial dome. The Great Square of Pegasus appeared over the eastern horizon as we settled into our cozy two-person sleeping bag and made the tent flaps fly.

The next morning, I awoke to the light streaming into our tent. I looked over at Frank, and he was leaning against his elbow, staring at me with a smile on his face.

"Hello, beautiful," he said.

"Good morning, handsome," I replied as he leaned over and kissed me.

After working up an appetite, we devoured a meal of Wonder Bread, peanut butter, and jelly. It was noon by the time we broke camp. The Ford trundled along in low gear as we plunged into the Shenandoah Valley limestones, then gained and lost altitude along Paleozoic valleys and ridges. From high on the Appalachian Plateau, we viewed the coal and shale beds in the roadcuts, now as familiar to Frank as the back of his hand.

Bypassing steel towns, we crossed the Central Lowlands toward Columbus, Dayton, and Indianapolis, skirting the edge of the anticlinal Cincinnati Arch below, capped by its Ordovician carbonates. North to Chicago, where we drove down Lake Shore Drive to take in the girls in macrame bikinis draped around beatniks strumming guitars in the sand. We headed toward Cedar Rapids in the midwestern heat, turned northward after a million cornfields, and aimed for Minneapolis. Northwestward over Minnesota's lake-dimpled landscape, we camped along the Otter Tail River as golden eagles soared overhead. The next day we crossed the state line and entered North Dakota without fanfare.

"I've got to pull over for gas," Frank said as he steered into a roadside gas station outside Fargo and pulled up to the pump. A young man in coveralls walked out of the garage bay and leaned over at Frank's open window.

"Fill her up, sir?"

Frank replied in the affirmative as I extracted myself from the front seat. My stiff legs crossed the pavement toward the facilities on the side of the building. Overhead, the oval Esso sign swayed and creaked in the tepid breeze. When I emerged, the attendant and Frank were examining the oil stick beneath the raised car hood.

"Oil looks good, sir," the man said, replacing the stick and slamming down the hood. He reached into his pocket and pulled out a fist-sized object. "Here you go, ma'am," he said, handing it to me as I approached. I looked down. It was a small juice glass, decorated with blue and red flags. "You can collect the whole set."

I thanked the man and climbed back into our car, glass in hand. A first souvenir of North Dakota.

Frank paid the attendant and slid back behind the wheel. "Thirty-two cents a gallon," he grumbled. "Highway robbery."

The ignition flared once more and we coasted back onto the highway. Traversing the High Plains with its cattle and wheat, we flew with no speed limit across the state until we approached the exit for Dickerson. After hours of staring into the blazing afternoon sun, my head pounded like a stampede.

"Do you want to drive around the town of Dickerson while we're here?" Frank asked, indicating the exit sign.

I shook my head. "No, honestly I just want to get to our house and move in. We can come back another day."

After four years of living apart, the prospect of moving into our own place felt like paradise. No more stolen weekends every six weeks, sneaking up the back steps of Frank's boardinghouse. I was sick of sharing space in the women's graduate dorm with a rotating assortment of library science majors. I hoped to never hear another discussion about the merits of the Dewey Decimal System ever again.

Frank stepped on the accelerator and we sailed onward. The plain stretched ahead, more grassland than I had ever imagined. After an hour of nothing else, a few buildings came into view in the distance.

"Do you think that's the town?" I asked, squinting through the windshield. "It's a pretty long drive into Dickerson from here."

"It must be. We haven't passed anything else."

"Yeah, or seen one other car," I said. "Calling this road a 'highway' is certainly a misnomer."

Frank slowed the car as we approached the clump of buildings bordering the road. A rusted sign indicated MAMMOTH, POPULATION 57.

Frank pointed. "Far out. This is it—our new town." He looked over to see my reaction.

I took in the scene on both sides of the road and tried to maintain a neutral expression. A wary feeling settled in my chest.

"It's far out all right," I said. "Not necessarily in a good way. The name's sort of an oxymoron, isn't it? Maybe they should have named it Minuscule."

A structure came into view on the right, the size of a double-wide trailer. CLARA'S BAR AND GRILL declared a sign in front of its aluminum-sided exterior. Next, a worn brick building housed the First Bank of the Dakotas. Across from the bank sat a tiny post office hut, the requisite American flag drooping on a pole, seemingly despondent in the windless air. One paved street bisected the highway. Down this street to the right, several low buildings were aligned parallel, like soldiers during an inspection. Signs indicated USED BOOKS and TINY'S BARBERSHOP.

We turned left onto the cracked asphalt of the side street, past an empty playground hosting a swing set, slide, and monkey bars rooted into parched dirt. Our car crawled down the road through what I assumed was the residential part of Mammoth. Houses in varying degrees of upkeep, none new, squatted on widely spaced lots. Several clapboard structures appeared abandoned, their roofs sagging, porches shrouded in overgrown goldenrod and tall grass. A few signs of habitation could be seen at other, mostly brick ranch-style homes—laundry drying on clotheslines or cars parked in yards.

Spying a driveway marked on either side with two ancient wagon wheels, Frank slowed to a crawl and turned in. We stared at the sad little bungalow in front of us. My heart whimpered.

"Home sweet home," Frank said.

I took a deep breath. "Well, I've seen worse," I said.

"You've lived in a tent. With a monkey," Frank replied.

"Exactly."

Winter winds had sandblasted the yellow-brick facade of the one-story house into a flaccid shade of flax. Small windows framed a central door on each side like weeping eyes. A pane in the left window was cracked and taped. The house had an attached one-car garage, its door standing crookedly ajar. Weeds pierced a concrete front walkway like arthritic fingers, and the overgrown turf in the yard could have fed a small herd of cattle. One scraggly cottonwood tree sheltered on the far side in the home's shadow.

Frank turned off the engine, and we climbed out of the car. I stood for a moment and inhaled the parched, oven-like air. A mosquito buzzed annoyingly in my ear. I reached up and swatted it away.

"The door is supposed to be unlocked," Frank said.

"Sure, why not?" I replied. "Who'd want to break in?"

Would I possibly be happy here, an East Coast girl in this corner of the desolate desert?

———

The next day we decided to explore our one-horse town. Or was it a half-horse town? The interior of our new home was complicit in our desire to leave it, the dilapidated furnishings outdone only by the sprinkling indicative of a mouse infestation. After scrubbing all morning, we set off, raw-handed, from our palatial abode, field hats on our heads, strolling through what loosely might be called "our neighborhood." Grasses waved in a faint breeze. Nothing else waved, as we saw no one. A baby wailed from inside a house. Past the empty playground, we turned at the intersection and entered the tiny post office. A middle-aged woman was behind a counter, sorting mail into cubbyholes.

"Good morning," Frank began. "We're . . ."

She looked over her shoulder, and a big grin bloomed across her face. "Oh, you must be the Baileys. Welcome to Mammoth! I have a piece of mail for you. A letter came for you already, don't ya know."

She pulled a letter out of a slot and offered it to me. "Here ya go. It's so nice to see some new faces. I sure do hope you like our town. You can ask me any questions you might have, and I'll try to help. But listen to me, goin' on. I'm Ada Swenson. I'm the postmistress here. Anything you need, just let me know, okay?"

"Thank you, Ada," I said, taking the letter from her. I looked at it. "Ah, it's from my mother. Anyway, I'm Henrietta and this is my husband, Frank. We just moved in yesterday."

"So pleased to meet cha. And I know. I saw you turn the corner in your car, loaded for bear. Nothing much gets past me."

"Do you live in town?" I asked.

"No, our place is farther out." She waved westward. "I'm born and raised in these parts, though. Never saw no reason to go anywhere else. Well, other than Montana, maybe. We head to Dickerson for entertainment every now and then. And church on Sundays, of course."

"Of course," I said, nodding. "We're just taking a walk around town. Anything we should see?"

She laughed and swiped a gray strand of hair off her forehead. "Well, that won't take ya long. If you're thirsty, you can get a pop at Clara's. She's also got bottles of milk in the cold box if you need one. It comes in handy in the winter, if ya can't make it to Dickerson for groceries. The used bookstore is open on a whim, so I don't know if that means today." She looked toward Frank. "You can get your haircut at Tiny's when you need it. Across from him is the bunkhouse. Mostly truckers stay there. At the end of the road, there's a path down to the river."

Frank pointed to the newspaper box in the corner. "I see we can get the newspaper here."

She nodded. "Yup. The *Dickerson Press*. Prints every Wednesday and Saturday. It's usually here by the afternoon."

Frank pulled some change out of his pocket and sorted it in his palm. Plucking out a dime, he fed it into the coin slot, causing the door to clonk as it unlocked. He pulled the glass front open, reached in, and grabbed a paper.

We thanked her and left. Frank handed me the paper. "Here you go. All the news that's fit to print."

I looked down and read aloud the front page headlines. "'Gemini 10 Reaches Highest Point in Space. American Troops in Vietnam Reach 500,000.'" I flipped the paper over. "And the equally important, 'Saucer Cited as Evidence of Outer Space Visitors.'"

"Well, that'll give us something to do at night. Other than the obvious." Frank smirked at me. "We can look for aliens in flying saucers. I'm sure if aliens wanted to visit Earth, they'd pick Mammoth as a landing site."

I laughed. "Yep, this would be the place." We crossed Main Street—no sign of any traffic in either direction—and walked past the bank.

"Let's go into the bank on the way back and make an appointment. We should open a joint checking account," Frank said.

"Wow, our first joint account," I said, smiling up at him. "Are you sure you trust me with your money?"

"I guess we'll find out," he said.

A crumbling sidewalk fronted the one-story buildings on the right. Their wooden exteriors had seen better days. Paint chips exfoliated into the breeze. We peeked through the window at the used bookstore.

"I can't see anything through this window. It's pitch dark inside," I said.

"No hours posted on the door." Frank tried the doorknob. "It's locked. I wonder how you know when it's open."

"There was a folding sign on the sidewalk yesterday. I saw it when we drove in."

Next door, Tiny's Barbershop appeared equally as vacant. A sign in the window indicated OPEN SATURDAYS.

Across the street, an old two-story Victorian house languished in the sun. It was in desperate need of attention, its wooden siding blemished with rot. "That must be the bunkhouse," I said.

"I guess so," Frank said. "Needs paint."

"Paint? How about a bulldozer?" I said.

Frank chuckled. "Want to walk to the river?"

"Sure."

The road dead-ended at a rusted metal guardrail. A well-worn path to the left cut across the prairie grass beyond. We followed the path, the land dipping slightly as we trod along, Frank leading the way. The air was so dry the skin on my arms felt itchy. Wrens flitted among the sedges, and crickets chirped in disharmony. The grasses formed seeding tasseled heads. We pushed them aside as we walked past, like reverse-threading a needle. I needed to learn the different varieties of plants here, I decided.

We emerged at the Little Missouri River, wide and tumbling, its waters rushing over well-worn rocks on its journey northward. Bushy willow trees grew along the far bank, leaves rustling softly. Two young boys fished along the bank, their bare feet squished in the muddy alluvium. One cast his line into the middle of the stream.

Frank waved to them. "How's the fishing?"

They looked at us like we were space aliens. One finally answered, "Oh, pretty good."

"What are you fishing for?"

"Walleye."

"Walleye?"

"Yeah. They're good eatin', I'll tell you that. Caught a few yesterday."

"Good luck," Frank said. We left them to their fish and walked away along the water's edge. The soft gurgling of the stream was mesmerizing. Our movement disturbed a crayfish, and it slid from its mudhole, disappearing into the current. Farther downstream, a pair of coots dove below the surface. I inhaled the sweet odor of marsh and mud.

"Want to stick your feet in?" Frank asked me.

"Okay, why not?" Setting the newspaper in the grass, I climbed up onto a flat-topped boulder at the water's edge. I pulled off my tennis shoes and socks, wiggling my freed toes. Frank joined me and knelt to untie his shoes.

"Go ahead," he said. "I'm right behind you."

I looked down into the swirling river, the water so transparent I could see all the rocks on the bottom. I lowered myself off the boulder and stepped with both feet into the stream.

The second my feet hit the water, a shock wave reverberated up my legs. My eyes jolted open. The water was numbingly cold. Frigid, on the cusp of glacial.

In addition to the biting cold, the transparency of the water had formed an optical illusion. What I thought was an ankle-deep step turned out to be a deep hole. I was submerged above my knees, the legs of my pedal pushers now soaked.

"Oh. My. God!" I shrieked, wrapping my arms around my torso.

Frank belly-laughed from his perch on the boulder. "Didn't you think the water would be cold?"

I managed to turn around toward him, teeth chattering. I cupped my hands into a scoop, gathered icy water in them, and threw it at him. He dodged and, still laughing, extended an arm out toward me. "Come on, grab my hand."

I grasped his hand, and he tried to lift me out of the water. The angle was wrong, the boulder was slippery, and smooth stones rolled under my feet. He pulled. I slipped forward and back. The next thing I knew, he flew into the river, headfirst, splashing down next to me like a gigantic snapping turtle. Then we were both in the water, shouting, laughing, and shivering.

The boys who were fishing probably thought we were aliens indeed.

It was a wet walk home.

CHAPTER 4

The next week, Frank started his new job, escaping to Dickerson and taking our car with him. I decided to hike into town and try the bookstore again. The folding sign was there this time, perched on the decaying sidewalk. USED BOOKS. I wrenched open the door, which gave an arthritic groan, and slid inside. A bell jingled over my head.

Sunlight filtered through the dirt-encrusted window illuminating dust motes floating in the stale air. The moldering scent of old paper mixed with stale tobacco. Metal bookcases lined up parallel, displaying books crammed willy-nilly on the shelves. Boxes in corners spilled with hardbacks.

A diminutive woman stepped through a back door. Her backbone was ramrod straight as she stood in worn jeans and a plaid shirt. Two long plaits of gray hair reached past her shoulders. Her sun-damaged complexion made it impossible for me to estimate her age, somewhere between sixty and eighty, I guessed. Her black eyes stared down at me over her aquiline nose. "Haven't seen you in here before," she said in a raspy voice.

"No, I've just moved into town," I replied.

She studied me, the lines around her eyes deepening. "Look around. The books aren't organized in any way." She waved at the shelves with her hand. Turning her back to me, she walked over to a box in the back and began to pull out books, one by one, examining the spines.

I meandered over to the shelves. She had not been kidding about the lack of organization. The books were stacked with no rhyme or reason. A few sported new covers, but most were worn and faded. I reached up, pulled out a book, and read the jacket. I picked up another. And a third. Excitement built in my chest. What a treasure trove! Some of my trepidation about living in this tiny town, with the specter of a North Dakota winter hovering over my head, seeped away.

Arms full, I walked over to a cash register resting on a decrepit desk. The woman sauntered from the back, cleared her throat, and inspected my selections. *The Spy Who Came in from the Cold. Dune. Cat's Cradle.* She made a sound that might have indicated approval.

"I was hoping to find a book on the plants of North Dakota. Do you have anything like that?" I asked.

She shook her head. "I will look. Come back again."

"Okay."

I dug coins out of my purse. "I'm Henrietta, by the way," I said.

She took my money and shoved the stack toward me. "We don't have any bags."

Our conversation over, her eyes followed my progress as I exited the store. I stood rooted on the sidewalk like a misplaced magnolia. Wow, I thought, she sure was blunt. Of course, people tended to say the same thing about me.

Frank turned eastward off the highway, and we rumbled down a dirt road, our station wagon bouncing and rolling across the ruts. Two weeks had passed, and we were ready to explore the badlands. The road ended at an impassable washout.

"Looks like this is as far as we go," Frank said. "I think we'd bottom out if we tried to cross that." He pulled over, turned off the engine, and we climbed out.

The wide expanse of the prairie stood in front of us, with the knolls of the badlands shimmering in the far distance. Occasional cumulus clouds lofted across the boundless turquoise sky. The sun on my face, adventure ahead, bliss settled into my chest.

"Your boss owns all this land?" I asked, gazing out at the scene in front of us.

"He owns all the flat land," Frank said, unfolding a topographic map and spreading it out on the car hood. He pointed at the contour lines. "I think we're parked here, next to this gully. See the hilly part to the west? That's all badlands, which is government land. BLM. Bureau of Land Management. We can hike anywhere around here."

"And we can collect fossils on BLM land?"

"We can collect fossils off the ground on BLM land. But we aren't allowed to dig without a permit." Frank opened the back door. "Let's grab our packs and lunch. I've got my canteen. Do you have yours? It's truly a desert out here."

"Got it. Do you have the compass?"

"Yep."

Leaving behind our dust-coated car, we plunged onto the plain, knee-high reeds attacking our pants. The blades waved a welcome in a light breeze as we trudged forward.

"Be sure to watch out for rattlesnakes," Frank said.

"Oh, I will," I replied with a shiver, looking down at my feet. "I have no desire to tangle with a snake again."

A previous encounter with a snake in Africa still gave me nightmares.

I continued, "Does your boss own cattle? Is that what he uses the land for?"

"I think so. Although I don't see any."

We walked along in companionable silence, the rustling of our boots the only sound except for an occasional far-off bird call.

"Is this what your field area looks like?" I asked. "Flat and grassy?"

Frank had already been sent to a rig during his first week of work.

"Yeah, pretty much. Without the badlands backdrop. Of course, it's an oil field, so there are wellheads and rigs and pumpjacks."

"Maybe you could take me to see it sometime?" I asked.

Frank shook his head. "I don't think so. Visitors aren't allowed."

I sighed. "What about just to observe? Even from a distance? Could I ride along and sit in the car?"

"We'll see. Don't hold your breath," he said. He pointed into the distance. "Let's hike to that peak over there."

Across the prairie, the spooky peaks of the badlands leaped vertically out of the earth. The gray spires mimicked fairy drip castles on an ancient shore. Surrounding the spiky pinnacles, heavily eroded mounds were incised by vertical gullies. The early morning sun washed the ashen strata with a tawny tinge, the grays and tans shining in an otherworldly glow.

"The badlands have a unique beauty, don't they?" I asked. "They look like water was poured over ancient ruins in an apocalyptic flood."

Frank smirked. "Wow. Poetic."

"Just call me Emily Dickinson," I said.

"Emily Dickinson? 'Wild Nights—Wild Nights!'" he said.

A faux-shocked expression crossed my face as I stared up at him. "You know Emily Dickinson?"

He clutched his palm to his chest. "You're wounding me here. I did go to Princeton, you know. I'm not a total Neanderthal."

He reached down and grabbed my hand and we continued, swinging our clasped fists, my heart light.

The turf thinned, transitioning to patchy rooted bundles. Thistles poked their spiny heads above the reeds. Prickly cactus pads bloomed pale lemon blossoms, which flounced in the breeze.

"Look, that cactus is blooming," I said, stooping to examine the delicate flowers. "I need to get a book on plants of the Great Plains."

"It's a cactus. What more do you need to know?" Frank asked.

"Well, a lot," I said, my eyes intent as I brushed apart the golden stamens carefully with one finger. "There are over one hundred genera in the family Cactaceae. Which species is this? What are the pollinators? Where . . ." I looked up at Frank and saw him grinning ear to ear. "Oh, you're teasing me."

"You're just so easy to tease," he replied. I stood and gave his shoulder a quick swat.

The vegetation along the edge of the meadow feathered even more, interspersing with low piles of gravelly dirt. Motion caught my eye.

"What was that?" I asked, startled. "I saw something move."

We held still and waited. A furry head popped out of a hole to our right, looked around, and popped back in.

Frank laughed. "It's a prairie dog. Look, there's a bunch of 'em."

"Oh yeah, I see their holes now. Remember when we saw them in Utah? On the Princeton trip?"

"Yeah, they were all over the place."

As we watched, rodent heads appeared and disappeared into the ground, black eyes on alert. A few brave animals climbed in and out of their holes, chubby brown bodies quivering. One large prairie dog squatted on his hind legs to glare at us. Paws at his chest, he trilled a series of loud warning barks.

Chu-rp, chu-rp, chu-rp, chu-rp.

"I guess he's the nonwelcoming committee," I said. "Let's hope the rest of North Dakota doesn't prove to be this hostile."

We arrived at the badland escarpment that rose at our feet like a king on his throne, stretching fifty feet toward the sky. I reached out and leaned against the rocks. The horizontal layers evidenced sedimentary rocks, each color denoting different lithologies. Drab siltstones and tan shales. Softened gray volcanic ash. Thin erosional runnels ran vertically, giving the hill its distinctive etched look. We knelt at its base as if in worship and set down our knapsacks. Frank opened his canteen and took a swig.

"Drink some water," he said. "You don't want to get dehydrated."

I pulled out my canteen and sipped. The lukewarm water washed down my parched throat. I pointed at the base of the cliff in front of us. "I'll start exploring these major erosional deposits. If there are fossils in the layers, maybe some were carried downhill by gravity or water."

Frank smirked. "All right, Eagle Eye. I'll scan the layers above you."

He took another long gulp and stowed the canteen back in his knapsack while I strapped mine around my neck and shoulder. We began a slow walk along the cliff, rock hammers in our hands. I focused on the small alluvial fans formed during infrequent rainstorms. The sediment was loose and gritty, and my boots slid in places. I leaned against the cliff with one hand, bending to examine each pile, sometimes sifting through the talus with my hammer. Frank stood upright, examining the horizontal strata with equal concentration. We worked silently, in tandem. Between the two of us, meandering along, we covered a fair bit of ground, both horizontally and vertically.

An odd textured pattern caught my eye. "Oh, look," I said, reaching down. "I think this might be a piece of fossil turtle shell." I held up a brown sliver in my fingertips and turned it in the sunlight. My pulse accelerated. "Yes, it is. See that reticulated pattern? This is definitely reptilian."

Frank came over and examined my find. "Far out," he said. "I would have walked right over that."

"You *did* walk over it," I said, raising an eyebrow. "Let me sift through this pile and see if I find any more." I pushed the gravel aside with my hammer. "See here? They're more pieces," I said, excitement rising in my voice. I bent and picked them up. "I know these are just 'float'—remains on the ground—but I still think they're interesting." I grinned and handed one to Frank.

"They must be Cretaceous," he said, turning it over in his hand. "This is all Hell Creek Formation as far as I know."

"A sixty-five-million-year-old turtle. It's amazing how the turtles survived the mass extinction, but all the dinosaurs died out," I said. "Such a mystery."

"Maybe you'll be the one to solve it," Frank said.

"Maybe we'll solve it together," I responded. My smile widened across my face.

The sun crossed the meridian, and heat seared my arms. Our sandwiches rested in our stomachs, and our water was almost depleted. Time to head back. We hiked a hypotenuse across the plain to the car rather than retracing our steps. I studied my feet, on the lookout again for rattlesnakes. Frank stopped next to me and bent down to the ground. "What's this?" he asked, picking something up. "Looks like a tooth." He handed the specimen to me.

I examined it, flipping it in my palm. The enamel glinted in the sunlight.

"Yep, it's a tooth all right. High-crowned with a double root. It's the tooth of a grazer. See the way the enamel loops on the top surface?" I showed Frank. "Animals that chew grasses evolved this pattern. The silica in the grass wears down the enamel, so this swirling on the top of the tooth adds extra enamel, which gives it more strength."

"Do you think it's a fossil?" Frank asked.

"No, not out here. Large mammals wouldn't be found in these strata. Plus the condition of the tooth is too pristine. If we were in Africa, I'd say it was an antelope tooth. Rhino teeth are more robust than this. And elephant teeth are enormous."

"What about out here?"

"I don't think horse teeth have this double root. My guess would be a cow tooth. Or a buffalo tooth, if there are any of those out here. They would both be about the same size, I think."

He pondered for a moment. "I thought the settlers killed most of the buffalo. Shot them from trains. To starve out the Indians."

A shiver ran through me, even in the warmth of the sun.

By late afternoon, we arrived back at our car, sweaty and tired, our arms scratched from crossing the reeds. My feet complained inside my boots, and my shoulders ached from the weight of my knapsack. But my face held a satisfied smile from the success of the hunt.

Frank walked around to the driver's side door and unlocked it, reaching inside for the extra thermos of water we had left in the car. Unscrewing the top, he rounded the hood again and offered it to me.

"Here, drink this," he said. I grabbed it and took a big gulp.

"Ugh, that water's hot," I said. "I can't believe we drank all of the water we carried. I thought we had plenty with us." I handed the thermos back to him.

He lifted it to his mouth and took a large swallow. "Yeah, next time we'll know to bring more," he said, wiping his mouth with the back of his hand.

As we jettisoned our knapsacks off our backs, a rumbling sound evidenced a car approaching in the distance. I squinted from the roadside into the late-day sun. The car drew closer and slowed.

"Looks like we've got company," Frank said.

A white four-door sedan pulled up behind us, its headlights on. The words BUREAU OF LAND MANAGEMENT were emblazoned on the side door. A single blue light strobed on the roof. Engine fumes filled our nostrils as we stood in the sweltering heat, staring at the car like it was a mirage. The driver's door opened and a man stepped out. He was dressed in full uniform, with his badge pinned to his tan shirt. A gun rested in a holster on his hip.

"Good afternoon," Frank said.

The officer analyzed us from beneath his brimmed hat. "Afternoon. Bureau of Land Management," he said by way of identification. He walked closer, one hand on his hip above the gun. "Can I ask what you two are doing out here in the middle of nowhere?"

"We're hiking," Frank replied.

The officer turned his bulldog face toward me. "Is that right, ma'am?"

"Yes, that's right," I said. "We hiked over to the badlands and back."

"You're a long way from the main road. And it's awfully hot out here for a hike."

"Yes, it was," Frank said as I nodded in agreement.

"There aren't any hiking trails out there," he said. "That I know of."

"No, we hiked across the plain," Frank said, meeting his eyes.

He returned Frank's stare. "Can I see some identification, please, sir?"

Frank dug into his knapsack and pulled out his wallet. He extracted his driver's license and handed it over.

The officer examined it and handed it back. "Virginia, huh? You're a long way from home, Mr. Bailey."

"We just moved to Mammoth," Frank said. "I'm a geologist with Monroe Petroleum."

This statement did nothing to thaw our chilly reception. The officer crossed his arms in front of his chest. "We've heard reports of poaching around here. Know anything about that?"

"Poaching?" I said. "Like shooting animals?"

He turned to me. "There's all sorts of poaching, ma'am."

"We don't know anything about poachers," Frank said.

"Would you mind opening the back of your car, Mr. Bailey, so I can look inside?"

Frank walked to the back of the station wagon, his boots kicking up miniature dust devils of dirt. He unlatched the tailgate, swinging it open with a loud creak. Several empty moving boxes still occupied the interior of our car.

The officer stepped around the door and peered inside. "What's inside the boxes?"

"Nothing. They're empty."

"Can you please pull them out, sir?" he asked.

I could see the steam beginning to rise from Frank as he reached inside and pulled out the boxes, one by one. They landed on the ground with a thud. The officer examined each one.

"All right," he said. He looked over at me. "What's in your knapsack, ma'am?"

"My knapsack?" I asked. "A canteen, rock hammer, a couple of fossils I found . . ."

"Fossils? What sort of fossils?" he asked, his voice sharpening like a razor.

"A few pieces of turtle shell. And we found a tooth. Although I don't think it's a fossil." I leaned down and picked my knapsack up off the ground. Unzipping the top, I held it out toward him. "Do you want to see them?"

"Please empty your knapsack. Everything on the ground."

I turned my knapsack upside down and dumped the contents in the dirt. I picked up the canvas sample bag containing the specimens and shook them out into my hand.

"These are fossil turtle shell pieces," I said, handing them over. "And here is the tooth."

The officer took a moment to examine them. "Did you dig for these?" he asked.

"No, sir," I answered. "We picked them up off the ground."

He handed the fossils and tooth back to me. "What are you going to do with them?"

My brow knitted. "Keep them for my collection."

He turned to Frank. "Now you, sir. Please empty your knapsack onto the ground."

Frank's face looked like thunder. "What's all this about?" he asked.

"Now." The officer's tone brokered no argument.

Frank grabbed his knapsack and turned it upside down. The contents spilled out—canteen, rock hammer, map, compass, extra sample bags.

The officer examined the sample bags to ensure they were empty. Picking up the hammer, he turned it over in his palm. "You know, there's a thin line between hammering and digging." He set the hammer back on the ground, his mouth a straight line. "Did you see anyone else while you were out here? Hiking around?"

"No, sir," Frank said, his nostrils flaring.

"Did you see any signs that someone had been digging in the badlands?"

"No, none."

"All right. I'll let you get on your way," the officer said. "But keep in mind, there are a lot of predators lurking in this area. You don't want to do too much wandering around. You never know what kind of trouble you might find yourselves in."

With a fishtail of gravel and clouds of silt, his car retreated. My hands shook as I picked up my belongings from the ground. Our tailgate slammed shut after Frank tossed the boxes back in the car. We slid into the front seat.

"What do you think that was all about?" I asked Frank.

He sat for a moment, staring out the windshield. "I don't know. Either that asshole wanted to harass a couple of greenhorns, or he's looking for somebody."

"I can't imagine there are many animals out here for poachers to shoot, can you?" I asked. "All we saw were prairie dogs."

"I don't think it's that. He was too concerned about what was in our knapsacks and whether we were digging. I have a feeling someone's been digging out here without a permit."

The engine roared, and Frank shifted the car into gear and swiveled the steering wheel to make a U-turn. We followed the police car's settling dust trail and headed toward home. Weary from the day's events, I slumped back into the car seat. "Well, I hope we get to come back," I said. "Hiking out here and finding my first North Dakota fossils has been the most excitement I've had in a while."

I bit my lip the minute those words escaped.

Frank glanced over at me and shook his head. "You mean, other than our wedding. And our honeymoon, right?"

Why did I always lead with my mouth instead of my head?

CHAPTER 5

Our kitchen table was now my office, the Formica top covered with envelopes, white typing paper, and my mimeographed résumés. Frank's manual typewriter sat on one end. I perched on a plastic chair and sipped coffee from a cracked mug. Yesterday's edition of the *Dickerson Press* was spread in front of me. I paged through the paper to the Help Wanted pages and picked up a pen. *Wanted: petroleum geologist, experience necessary.* Hmm. *Wanted: Oil field service company seeks field specialist. Wanted: Driller, experience necessary. Wanted: Mud logger, will train.* I circled them all.

Frank crossed the kitchen, tying his tie around his neck. He leaned over my shoulder. "Henrietta, you're wasting your time. None of those companies are going to hire a woman. And you aren't qualified for most of these jobs. They want someone with experience."

I raised my eyebrows at him and frowned. I had been typing cover letters all week, adding them to my résumé. My first envelopes were ready to mail. I pursed my lips. "How do you know? Besides, I can't just sit around all day. I may as well *try* to apply."

I set the newspaper down and pulled the stack of envelopes toward me.

Frank let out a long breath. "Would you even *want* to do this kind of work? It's not so bad going to oil wells now, but wait until winter sets in. You know they keep drilling in the winter, right? Time is money. When it's twenty below zero, are you going to want to be sitting in a trailer at a rig? For days at a time?"

I picked up a page of stamps and tore one from the corner. "I don't know. You won't take me to see a rig, so I have no idea what it's like." I licked the back of the stamp and stabbed it onto the corner of the top envelope.

Frank threw his hands in the air. "You're being unreasonable, you know. I could get fired for taking you."

"Would you have to tell anyone? Can't you sneak me in?"

"It's not like the rig is ever abandoned. Someone's always there."

"Maybe you could try to think of something."

"You know, I thought you might be happy to have some time off. You'd been working hard on your PhD for so long. Maybe you deserve a break."

"And do what exactly? Cook and clean the house?"

"Well, yeah . . . would that be so bad? Take a break and relax. And I thought maybe we could talk about having kids. We aren't getting any younger, you know."

A red haze clouded my vision. I rose slowly from my chair. My jaw clenched.

"Kids? Do you know me at all? Did you listen to me for the past four years? While I was struggling to finish my degree? Did you hear when I told you about how the only time I could reserve the electron microscope seemed to be at midnight? Every. Single. Time. Did you listen when I complained about how my adviser made me hand-draw every pollen grain? To scale? Even though we had the technology to photograph them?"

Frank tried to answer, but I gulped another breath and kept going.

"Do you remember when, during my last year, my committee suddenly decided I needed to take a second year of physics? Because I had only taken one year in undergrad? Another year of physics so that I could become a paleontologist? Two more semesters, when I was trying to write the final draft of my dissertation?"

"Yeah, I remem—"

"Remember how they nitpicked over my statistics? Arguing among themselves? I had to redo the math, and then, when all was said and done, I ended up having it correct the first time?"

"Okay . . ."

"Did you listen to me, raving on the phone late at night, about how my committee would change just a few words in every draft so I had to retype entire chapters over and over? To get the final document to be perfect?"

"I had to do that too, you know," he said.

"Then you should know, how after all of that, the last thing I'd want to do is 'take a break and relax.' The last thing I'd want to do after all of that work is to stay home and have a baby." Tears of frustration rimmed my eyes. "And I'm not that old. I'm only twenty-six."

Frank swiped his hand through his hair and let out another exasperated sigh. "I'm sorry. I didn't mean to get you all worked up. But think about it from my perspective. I'm thirty-two. I've been waiting a long time for us to start our lives together. You told me that we'd have kids someday. And I don't want to be in a wheelchair by the time they're in high school."

I studied his face. There was a yearning in his eyes I had not noticed before. And it frightened me. How could I have missed this? I was swimming in water over my head.

With a tight voice, I replied. "I don't remember saying *kids*, plural."

Frank opened the door leading into the garage. "We'll have to talk about this later. I've got to go to work." He slipped through the door, letting it bang closed behind him. I was left to stare at his retreating back. I forced the lump in my throat down with another swallow of coffee and stared blindly at the newsprint.

Our squabble was left to simmer that morning, like the boiling water beneath a geyser, ready to flash to steam.

Flowers, when presented with humbleness, can smooth over con-
flicts, assuage fears, and melt hearts, or so I have found. Like honey
poured over an open wound, when Frank came home that evening
and gifted me with a bouquet of sunflowers, I felt a sweet drizzle of
comfort spread over me like a balm.

"I'm sorry, babe," he said, presenting me with the paper-wrapped
bundle of sun-heads. "I didn't mean to pressure you this morning. I
understand how hard this is for you."

I grasped the blooms and sniffed, the subtle fragrance of the
sunflowers lifting to my nose. "Thank you," I said. "I appreciate that.
And the flowers are beautiful."

He gathered me into a bear hug, smushing the bouquet between
us. "You know I love you, and I'll help you in any way I can to find
a job." He kissed the top of my head. We rocked gently back and
forth, standing in the kitchen together as one ship navigating life's
tidal forces.

I raised my face to his. "Including taking me to a rig?"

He met my eyes, smiled his half smirk, and slowly shook his
head. "You don't give up, do you?" he asked in a gentle voice.

I returned his smile and did not answer. The question was rhe-
torical, after all.

Two weeks later, my hands were stuck in soapy dishwater when the
phone rang. I dried them on a tea towel as I hurried into the living
room and reached for the receiver.

"Hello?"

"Good morning," said a woman's voice. "I'm calling from
GeoCore Mudlogging, for Mr. H. B. Ballantine."

I sucked in a huge gulp of air. I had used the old trick of putting
my initials instead of my name on my résumé.

For once, my thoughts outraced my mouth. "May I ask why you
are calling?"

"Yes. I'm trying to set up a job interview for Mr. Ballantine with our recruiter, Mr. Herman Pody."

"What day and time?" I asked.

"Next Monday at ten o'clock."

"H. B. Ballantine will be at your office at ten next Monday," I said.

"Excellent." She rattled off the address. "Please ask Mr. Ballantine to bring several copies of his résumé."

"Yes indeed. Thank you."

I gently set the receiver back onto the base. Raising my arms in the air with a hoot, I danced the Twist around our sagging threadbare couch while croaking out the lyrics at the top of my lungs. Chubby Checker would be appalled. A better method to rid the house of vermin had yet to be invented. Any remaining mice scattered.

"We're heading out in five," Frank called to me from the living room as I shoved my feet into my boots and struggled to thread the long rawhide laces.

"Should I wear a hat, or will I need a hard hat?" I asked.

"Bring both. I don't know how close you'll be able to get to the rig. We're going to play this by ear."

"But you'll try to get me close, right?"

I followed Frank out the door. A few katydids sawed in the grass, marring the otherwise pristine stillness of the early morning. I inhaled deeply, the air tinged with the faraway scent of mowed grass. The July sun peeked in the east, painting the horizon with a banquet of apricot and tangerine streaks. We climbed into the car, and the slamming of the doors echoed, disrupting the quiet.

"Thank you again for taking me to the rig," I said. "I want to see what a mud logger does before my interview."

Frank glanced over at me as he turned on the ignition. "You don't have to keep thanking me. At least not yet. You may end up sitting in the car in the parking lot."

"I appreciate the effort." I leaned over and kissed his cheek.

He pulled the gearshift into drive without looking at me. "My impression of the oil business is that it's a lot like the coal business. A good ole boys' network. Roughnecks will tell you that women are bad luck at a rig."

I rolled my eyes. "I heard that years ago about the coal mine. It's all superstitious nonsense." I pressed my lips together and folded my arms across my chest.

"That's easy for you to say. But the beliefs are still out there."

Frank steered the car north to skirt the badlands and headed for the oil fields. I rolled down the window and felt the dry breeze buffet my face. Sunlight shimmered off the yellow-green grass that stretched to the horizon in all directions. Barbed wire fencing held back acres of grasslands, a few head of cattle dotting the landscape, unbothered and untended. No farmhouses were in sight. Cottonwood trees lined an occasional stream coursing across the prairie.

The radio played a mixture of static and scratchy polka tunes. After a half hour of that torture, I flipped off the racket. "Tell me about the Williston Basin," I said.

Frank cleared his throat. "What do you know about oil and gas?"

"I know you need a source rock with a high organic content, like a shale. It has to be buried, and the temperature has to be high enough to cook the organics into oil. The temperature is lower for oil than for natural gas."

"Yep, that's right," he said. "What else?"

"Once the oil or gas is generated it can migrate out of the source rock. It collects in rocks with high porosity and permeability. The reservoir rocks. Usually, there's an impermeable layer, a caprock, on top to prevent the oil or gas from escaping to the surface. But there also has to be a trap of some kind where the petroleum will lodge. The most common traps are faults, salt domes, or anticlines." I held my right hand up in an arch shape to emphasize an anticline.

"Good. The Williston Basin provides all of those conditions except salt domes. The basement rocks are Precambrian, and a weak zone within them allowed for a depression to form in the early Paleozoic."

I picked up the story. "A sea covered the area at that time, right? So the depression must have filled with marine sediments."

"Right again. The rocks are limestones, sandstones, siltstones. And lots of shales. Ages from Ordovician all the way to the Mississippian. Four hundred and eighty million years old, with deposition continuing for at least one hundred million years."

I smiled, picturing marine life here at that time. Horn corals, crinoids, and brachiopods anchored in the muck, filtering out microorganisms. Trilobites scurrying along the bottom, feeding on carrion. Cephalopods and armored fish swimming in the shallow sea.

Frank continued, "When the Laramide orogeny uplifted the whole area, the strata buckled into arched-shaped anticlines. These provided the traps. The prospect today is on the Little Knife anticline. We're drilling into limestones capped by anhydrite."

We turned onto a packed dirt road, bumping along, the sun now at our backs. Our tires left a fog of dust in our wake. Pumpjacks appeared in the distance, their mechanical heads grinding up and down, pumping oil from deep-seated reservoirs.

"There's the rig," Frank said. I felt my pulse quicken. Ahead, a steel derrick rose in the distance like a needle toward the sky.

"How deep will the well be?" I asked as I gripped the door handle.

"TD is fourteen thousand feet. That's total depth. We're halfway there. They're running logs today, which is why I'm here."

"To interpret the logs?"

"Exactly. And put in some face time. It'll be quiet here today. The roughnecks won't be here since we're logging. I'm not sure about the mud loggers. I'll see if I can get you past the company man."

The derrick grew larger as we bounced along. Cirrus clouds danced above it as if they had been painted with a steel brush.

"They bring all this equipment out here on trucks, I guess? Down this road?"

"Yep. It has washed out some since then. They might have to grade it before taking it all back out."

We parked in a gravel area and climbed out of the car. Frank grabbed his briefcase from the back seat, and we walked to the middle of the lot to stare up at the rig. The derrick rose at least a hundred feet into the air and rested on top of a massive steel substructure about thirty feet high.

"Up there's the drilling floor," Frank said, pointing to the base of the derrick. "And below that, on the ground under the platform, is the blowout preventer."

We walked to the far side of the site, our boots crunching on the gravel.

"I see they've trucked in a lot of stone."

"Oh yeah, there has to be a stable gravel pad for the rig. Since they're not drilling, the drill pipe is over here on the pipe deck. Let's walk over to the mud pit." We passed a rack with stacked thirty-foot lengths of pipe.

"Here's the mud pit." Frank pointed. "For the recirculated drilling mud."

The mud pit was aptly named, a huge rectangular depression, about five feet in depth. It was lined with plastic, which rose along the sides. A viscous brown ooze filled the bottom, emitting an earthy, somewhat metallic odor.

"What's in the mud?" I asked, crinkling my nose as I stared down into the pit.

"Clay. Usually bentonite, plus chemicals to increase its density. And lubricants. There are different types of mud, depending on what we're drilling through."

"What does the mud do?"

"The mud keeps the hole from collapsing and keeps any subsurface fluids from entering the well. It also helps control the pressure. And it cools the drill bit. The mud circulates down the middle of the drill pipe, comes out the bottom through the bit, and returns to the surface along the outside of the pipe. All the pieces of ground-up rock get carried to the surface in the mud. One of the mud logger's jobs is to take samples of the rock chips out of the mud. The chips are called 'cuttings.' The mud logger makes a stratigraphic column with the cuttings so we know what rocks we're drilling through."

"I could do that," I said, squinting up at him. "I've studied enough stratigraphy and analyzed plenty of cores at the Smithsonian."

"Sure you could. If you want a muddy job with long hours and little sleep."

I let that comment pass. "What does the geologist do?" I asked.

"Good question. I propose the well location and tell them how deep to drill. I keep track of the drilling progress. I correlate the logs from well to well in a field and across the basin. I examine the cuttings. I describe any rock cores. The bottom line—I analyze data."

"Ooh, I love data."

"I know you do, sweetie," he said, cracking his first smile of the day. "I know you do."

My heart warmed at that smile.

We walked back across the parking lot, passing a blue truck with SCHLUMBERGER painted on the side in white letters.

"What's Schlum-ber-ger?" I asked.

Frank chuckled. "It's French, and pronounced 'Schlum-ber-zhay.' It's the company that runs the logs."

"And what, exactly, are logs?" I asked.

"I'll show you," he said. "Come on."

A small metal trailer sat on-site, rusting in the sun. Frank scaled two metal steps to its front door and reached for the knob. The door was locked.

"The mud loggers must not be here today. This is their trailer. I guess they're taking a break while Schlumberger's here."

I felt a tug of disappointment. "That's too bad," I said. "I wanted to see their equipment."

"At least you got to see the mud pit. Let's go meet the company man. He's in charge of everything on the rig. Just follow my lead, and we'll see if he buys it."

Frank led me to a large construction trailer. We clanged up the metal stairs and entered. Sunlight fought a losing battle against the grime-filled windows, giving the inside a cave-like appearance. Dirt caked the floor. On one side, papers spilled across a table surrounded by four gray folding chairs. On the other side, behind a huge metal desk, a bearlike man looked up. He pushed out of his chair as we came through the door, wiping his hands on the front of his coveralls.

"How ya doin', Frank?" he said, reaching out a massive paw to shake Frank's hand. His attention swiveled to me and his eyebrows rose. "And who's this here?"

"Hey, Joe. This is Henrietta Ballantine," Frank said. "She's a consulting geologist from Washington, and I'm showing her the rig."

Joe looked at me with wary eyes, analyzing me like I was a Soviet spy in his trailer. "From Washington, huh? You mean Washington, DC or State?"

"DC. Thank you for allowing me to be here."

His frown deepened. "You're not with the government, are ya?"

"No, sir."

He turned to Frank. "Ya know, I didn't hear nothing about this from the office."

Frank nodded with a sage expression on his face. "It was last minute."

"Oo-kay, but no wandering around with her. Anybody else sees her, they'll blow a circuit."

"Yes, sir, absolutely. How's the logging going?"

Joe tore his gaze from me, cleared his throat, and pointed a meaty finger to a table in the corner. "Been going fine. Your logs are over there. Two of 'em anyway. Schlumberger's running the gamma ray now. Think I'll go check on 'em."

We shuffled over to the table as Joe banged out the door.

A cloud immediately lifted off Frank's face. "Well, that went better than I expected," he said as he unfurled a long ream of paper.

"He seemed all right," I said.

"At least he didn't shoo you out to the car."

We pulled up two metal folding chairs, and I stared down at the paper in front of us. Two sets of squiggly lines ran vertically along a continuous roll of paper. Depths were printed in the middle.

"The technicians lower tools down the hole to measure properties of the rock." Frank pointed at one of the curves on the page. "This curve on the left is the SP, or spontaneous potential, log. And this line on the right is the resistivity log. They both measure electrical properties. Look here at the SP log. This is the 'shale baseline.' There's lots of shale down there, but we're not drilling for that. When the SP curve deflects to the left of the baseline, the rocks are more permeable, either limestone or sandstone. That's what we're aiming for, because oil travels through permeable rocks. Each rock layer has a characteristic SP curve. I use those curves to correlate the formations across the oil field."

"Interesting. And the resistivity log?" I asked.

Frank's gestures became more animated as he explained his work to me. I could tell that the petroleum business suited him. And I was happy for him, truly.

He answered, "It measures the electrical resistivity of the formation, including the resistivity of the fluid in the pore spaces. Since oil doesn't conduct electricity, the resistivity log will show a large deflection if the pore spaces are filled with oil."

"Okay. And what's the gamma log that's being run now?"

"The gamma ray log indicates the amount of natural radiation in the rocks. Shale has a higher reading because of radioactive potassium in the clays. I use that curve to correlate too."

He set his briefcase on the table and opened it, retrieving another long ream of paper.

"This is the log from the nearest well. I'll set them alongside each other and see at what depths we're encountering the strata here, compared with the well to the north. If layers are missing in the log, it means we've crossed a fault."

He grabbed both logs and lined them up, sliding the pages against each other, matching the shapes of the squiggles, and marking the correlations with a pencil. I leaned back in my chair and observed. For the life of me, I could not figure out any reason a woman could not do this work. Other than superstition, chauvinism, bigotry, machoism, and fear of changing the status quo. The shale in the SP log was not the only thing that needed a shift from the baseline.

CHAPTER 6

The tepid August air blew through the open windows as we raced down the highway. An hour by car, Dickerson was the nearest town of any decent size in any direction. Our car headed there every weekday, taking Frank to work. By now, a month into our North Dakota pilgrimage, the station wagon could probably have steered itself to Dickerson.

The highway exit led us onto First Street. With a complete lack of imagination, the town's founding fathers numbered, rather than named, the roads. The even numbers ran east-west and odd numbers ran north-south, in a parallel grid. To get to the grocery store, Third Street ended at the Dakota Save Rite. Turn onto Eighth Avenue and find Pepper Pharmacy. The bowling alley could be found on Fifth. Driving past the movie theater on Second, the marquee advertised *Batman: The Movie* and *Who's Afraid of Virginia Woolf?*

A few spaces were empty as we pulled in front of the two-story cinder-block building housing Monroe Petroleum. Frank put the car into park, leaned over, and kissed me. "Good luck today," he said.

"Thanks, I may need it," I said, sliding across the seat to the driver's side as he climbed out of the car. He helped me pull the seat closer to the steering wheel. I grasped it with moistened palms. "I'll pick you up at five."

He walked over to the front door of his building, waved, and disappeared inside.

The sun glinted through the windshield, and I began to sweat in my skirt and jacket. My nylon stockings adhered to my legs like a second skin. I had an hour to wait until my interview, so I drove two blocks over, arriving at Four Seasons Park. Known for its World War II memorial, straight rows of linden trees ringed the grounds. I grabbed my copy of my latest book, *A Journal of the Plague Year* by Daniel Defoe, and settled on a park bench in the shade. Contemplating a deadly microorganism killing the entire population of the planet focused my attention away from my jitters, at least temporarily. Even if my interview did not go well, at least mankind wasn't being destroyed by a virulent plague.

Forty-five minutes later, I left my perch, drove to a low brick building, and parked out front. My heart began to ratchet in my chest as I approached the door with GEOCORE MUDLOGGING stenciled on its glass window. I pushed inside. A young receptionist, presumably the one who had telephoned me, looked up from her typewriter.

"May I help you?"

She was a pretty woman, wearing a blouse that was tighter than I thought necessary. I cleared my throat. "Yes. I'm Dr. Ballantine, here to see Mr. Herman Pody."

The woman, momentarily speechless, gaped at me, round-eyed.

"For an interview," I clarified.

"Um . . ." She looked down at her desk and shuffled some papers together. "Yes, well, just a minute." Rising from her chair, she tottered on high heels to a side door and knocked. "Mr. Pody?" she called out.

"Yes?" said a voice from within.

She cracked open his office door and stuck her head inside. "Your ten o'clock appointment is here."

"Thank you, Jean. Send him in."

Her smile froze on her face like a Halloween mask as she opened the door wider and beckoned for me to step inside.

"This way."

I thanked her and stepped across the threshold.

Mr. Pody, rising from his chair, gave the impression of an electrocuted inmate when he spotted me. His eyes held the petrified look of someone who had stepped on a copperhead. His hand already extended, he looked from me down to his arm. I could tell he was wondering whether to offer me a handshake. I stepped forward. "Hello, I'm Dr. H. B. Ballantine, but please call me Henrietta," I said, reaching out. I tried to shake his hand, but he compromised by squeezing mine before withdrawing his.

"How do you do. Please take a seat."

"I guess I'm not what you were expecting," I said as I smoothed my skirt and sat on the chair facing his metal desk. *May as well get that right out there.*

He lowered himself into his chair. "No, you are not." He shook his head back and forth. "Not at all. How did you hear about the job?"

"Through an ad in the *Dickerson Press*," I said.

"Ah, yes. Are you from Dickerson?" he asked.

I replied, "No, I'm from Virginia. My husband and I just moved to North Dakota."

"You're married?" he asked, his eyes traveling to my wedding ring.

"Yes."

"Do you have any children?"

"No, I do not."

"I see," he said, leaning his elbows on his desk and steepling his fingers under his chin. He looked down at his papers, my résumé resting on top. A minute lapsed while he picked it up and read over its contents. I studied the dust particles hovering in the sunrays pouring through his window. A large plastic plant in the corner sagged with neglect.

Mr. Pody cleared his throat with a phlegmy sound. "You have a PhD in geology?" he asked, as if I had lied on my résumé.

"Yes. In paleobotany, but I know a lot about sedimentary rocks."

"A bit overqualified, I'd say. Why would you want to be a mud logger? Do you know what a mud logger does?"

"I'm looking for a job to advance my career. I've done a lot of stratigraphic work. I know how to examine cuttings and cores. I can draw stratigraphic columns. And I wouldn't mind washing samples from the mud pit."

"How about when it's twenty below zero and the wind is howling?" he asked.

"I won't know until I try it," I said, trying to stare him down.

He paused again with a puzzled expression. I had the impression that wheels were spinning in his head. "Why are you in North Dakota of all places?"

"I'm here because my husband took a job with Monroe Petroleum. He's also a geologist."

A tidal wave of relief washed across his face. "Oh, we couldn't possibly hire you, then," he said. "We're contracted by a lot of different oil companies. It would be a conflict of interest for you to work for us."

"A conflict of interest?"

"Yes, you'd be exposed to proprietary information at different rigs. We couldn't have that passed along, even inadvertently, to your husband at Monroe."

A sense of loss began to work its way into my heart. I hadn't been prepared for that statement and couldn't come up with a quick reply. I sat, wordless, and pursed my lips.

Mr. Pody stood and smiled a big-toothed grin. "I'm so sorry," he said in a stilted voice. "It was a pleasure to meet you. Miss Evans will show you out."

I mimicked his smile like a mirror. "Thank you for taking the time to speak with me," I said.

"Not at all," he replied, his eyes already back on his papers.

Miss Evans was on her feet, holding the outer door open for me as I left. She smiled like a cat as I passed her. "Thank you for coming in," she said in a solicitous tone. As I slipped out the door, she muttered under her breath, "H. B.? What a hoot." I couldn't tell if she was laughing with me or criticizing me. The finality of the door clicking shut behind me felt like an omen.

I returned to my car, started the ignition, and backed out of my parking spot. Not thirty minutes had passed since I'd entered the building. With a lump of hopelessness in my throat, I headed for home. Ten minutes into my drive back to Mammoth, I let out a scream of frustration loud enough to startle all the coyotes within a twenty-mile radius. Then I allowed my pent-up tears to flow down my cheeks. It seemed there was no job market in North Dakota for a woman with a knowledge base of fossil pollen, leaves, seeds, clams, trilobites, and fish skeletons. Was I doomed to spend the approaching winter sequestered inside my house? For days on end? I might as well be quarantined from a deadly plague.

CHAPTER 7

Frank left for work as usual, fueled by coffee and with a satisfied smile on his face as if anticipating a birthday party. Left to my own devices, stranded without a car, I headed to the bookstore in hopes of finding it open for business. A bag of books to return weighed on my shoulder. The sun's rays strained behind a white cirrus haze, dimming the landscape as I walked. Bees thrummed in the weeds, anxious for late summer blooms. Grasshoppers congregated, whirring their slender wings. I passed the overgrown yards and abandoned bungalows, always unchanging, like stationary backdrops on a movie set. Reaching the vacant highway, I looked across and spotted the folding sign on the sidewalk. My spirits lifted. I hefted my bag and crossed the road. Reaching the door to the shop, the jingle of the overhead bell felt like winning the lottery.

Inside, I set my bag of books on the desk by the cash register. The diminished sunlight struggled to penetrate the grimy front window, casting shadows over the books. The stacks hovered around me like towering stalagmites in the grotto-like space. I browsed the selections, once again disquieted by the disarray. Several titles engaged me, and I began to collect them in my arms.

Without a sound, I felt a sudden prickle of someone at my back. I turned and there she was, watching me. The woman with the braids. A shiver ran up and down my arms.

"Hello," I said. "I'm so glad to see you're open today. Did you find a book on the local plants by any chance? I brought back the books from last time." I inclined my head toward the desk.

She drew a long, slow breath, her eyes penetrating mine. "I don't pay for returned books."

"Oh, no, that's all right."

She turned, walked over to a shelf, and plucked a book off the top. "Here, Henrietta. Your book on plants." She extended her arm and held the book out to me.

"You remembered my name," I said, a small smile forming on my lips. I looked down at the offering. *Botany of the Western States.* I reached for it, set it on top of my collection, and opened the cover. I flipped through a few of the pages. "This is perfect, thank you. I see there's a chapter on the High Plains."

She held out another book. "I thought you might need this as well."

I looked over and read the title. *Western Wildlife.* "Where do you get your books?" I asked.

"Different places. My people bring them to me."

"Your people?" I squinted at her. "Are you an American Indian?" She stared at me as if considering my question. I bit my lip and felt the blood rush up my cheeks. "I'm sorry if it's not polite to ask."

She exhaled a long breath before answering. "I am not from India," she said, slipping the second book on the top of my pile.

I swallowed the suddenly bitter taste in my mouth. "Oh, I know that. I meant, Native American?"

She paused again. "Why would I claim to be from a country named for a white explorer?"

"I don't know. I . . ."

"My name is Kima," she said. "You may call me Kima since we are now friends."

"That's a pretty name. Kima."

She nodded. "My name means 'butterfly on the wind.'"

Two more weeks passed with no more replies to my résumé, and a bitter realization settled into my bones. No one in the oil business was going to hire me as a geologist or anything remotely related. I shoved my stack of résumés into a drawer, slamming it shut. Instead, I decided I needed exercise and a new point of view.

After an early breakfast, I banged out the front door, walked down the driveway, and turned westward along the asphalt toward town. At the cross street, two mongrel dogs, one a sort of Labrador mix and the other a beagle mutt, lounged lazily in the middle of the road. The Labrador lifted his head and gave a perfunctory bark, then set his head back down with a sigh. My sentiments exactly. Arriving at the post office, I looked up and down the highway. An eighteen-wheeler rumbled toward me, and as it passed, the trucker sounded his air horn, a defeated, bellowing moan that echoed the feeling in my chest.

Across the highway, I passed the bank, currently bereft of customers. I peeked inside the bookstore's window, closed at this early hour—or almost any hour, since Kima's schedule was known only to herself—and continued past the barbershop, arriving at the dead end near the river. The footpath beckoned, and I treaded down it, the tall reeds on either side brushing my hands like coarse boar hairs. The path terminated and the Little Missouri appeared in front of me, its current rushing turbulently over glacial moraine. The outdoor scent of fresh mud and marshy vegetation hovered in the air. Two kicks and my shoes fled from my feet. I peeled off my socks and walked down to the water's edge. With ginger steps and a quick inhale to gird against the shock, I submerged my feet in the transparent, crystal water. The delicious iciness sent a shiver up my spine, contrasting with the warmth of the sun on my face. I basked for a few moments, alone except for a flock of foraging black terns. A ritualistic beginning to a vacant day of discontent.

Or so I thought.

I arrived back home to find a woman walking across my lawn, heading to my doorstep. I recognized her, having seen her from a distance several houses down. With her sturdy frame and long blonde hair, I could imagine her as one of the original pioneers crossing the prairie. Two small children, a boy and a girl, trailed after her, like ducklings in Boston Public Garden.

I waved to her from my driveway.

"Hello," she called out. She held up a plate covered in aluminum foil. "I brought you some kolaches. To welcome you to the neighborhood. I know I'm late . . ."

"That's so nice of you," I said as we approached my door simultaneously. "Huaraches? Aren't they a type of shoe?"

She looked at me quizzically. "No. Kolaches."

"Oh," I said. "Sure. Kolaches." I waited for a beat as I stared at the aluminum foil and tried to assess what was underneath. "What are kolaches?"

"They're cookies," she replied, a tentative look on her face. "I'm Janine. These are my children, Michael and Diane."

Diane piped up, tugging at the hem of her smocked dress. "We're twins."

I looked back and forth at the children. "I see that now. You look exactly alike."

Diane shook her pigtails. "No we don't. I'm a girl and Michael's a boy."

"Ah, yes, I stand corrected." I found myself smiling, despite my earlier mood. "I'm Henrietta," I said to Janine. I leaned over toward the children. "You can call me Mrs. Bailey."

"We're five years old," offered Michael.

"Please, come on in," I said, turning the doorknob.

"We don't want to take up your time . . ." Janine protested.

"Oh, no, please do. Maybe Michael and Diane can show me what a kolache looks like."

I pushed open the door and we trooped inside. It was the first time anyone other than Frank or I had been inside our home. With a critical eye, I scanned my living room, taking in the threadbare couch, lumpy chair, and dented coffee table.

"It's not fancy," I said.

"None of these houses are fancy," Janine said. "Did yours come furnished?"

"Yes. Heavens, I didn't pick out this awful furniture on purpose," I said.

She laughed. "Ours came furnished too. These places have been passed from one family to the next. Ours looks a lot like yours."

My cheeks warmed. "Not to say that your furniture is awful," I tried to backpedal and cleared my throat. "What I mean to say is . . . would you like some coffee?"

Diane blurted, "I'd like some apple juice, please."

Janine frowned at her daughter. "Diane, don't be rude."

She looked up at her mother, a little carbon copy. "I said 'please.'"

The weight in my chest lifted just a little. "Let's go into the kitchen. I have some apple juice in the refrigerator."

I was out of practice having a nonwork-related conversation. Four years had passed since my college days with easy access to my peer group, my Philomathean Society sisters. My graduate program had been full of male students. I had been the outlier. And I had been dating Frank. Once word spread that I had a boyfriend, any attention I had received early on stopped. Most of the men just ignored me. And to be honest, I ignored them. We formed a mutual aversion society. I had not gone to the university to be social anyway. Yet the past four years had come at a price, and that price had been my isolation for weeks on end.

But that morning, sitting in my kitchen with Janine, I tried to channel my mother's ability to chat easily with friends, and my loneliness seemed slightly less fraught. I found out that the twins had another year before they started first grade, they owned a cat named Stripes, and they were a "joyful handful." Janine's husband was a roughneck working on the oil rigs, and she was a full-time mother and homemaker.

And I discovered that kolaches were a yummy combination of folded dough, apricot jam filling, and powdered sugar. They were especially delicious when shared.

CHAPTER 8

Polka music blasted from a speaker, interrupted by the din of car horns. A metal bleacher bench beneath me, I leaned, elbows to knees, and stared at the unfolding scene through my dusty lenses. Dry heat rolled over the plains, chapping my lips and my skin. The rounded hills of the badlands stood in the far distance behind us, sparse vegetation crisping in the sun. September was rodeo time in western North Dakota, and Mammoth hosted one, held at the edge of town in a once-vacant lot.

The population swelled as people arrived from surrounding communities. Silt-enshrouded pickups parked parallel along the highway shoulder and filled the side streets. People scuffed along, arriving at the entrance where vendors sold popcorn, hot dogs, funnel cakes, and Pepsi. The scent of grease permeated the air, mixing with the dusky smell of horse manure and heifers. American flags hung listlessly in the air. Groups of teenagers loitered, taking in the scene, surreptitiously smoking cigarettes held behind bell-bottomed pants.

"Ladies and gentlemen," boomed the announcer. "Welcome to the Mammoth Rodeo! It's time for the opening parade!"

We applauded at the announcement. A color guard carried the American flag and the North Dakota state flag through the entrance, followed by a convertible and several open-backed pickup trucks.

The speaker's voice echoed across the bleachers. "Please welcome our master of ceremonies, Mr. George Monroe, with his lovely wife, Faye, a former Miss Rodeo America 1953."

The couple seated in the back seat of the convertible waved to the crowd. Frank pointed toward them. "That's my boss. George is the founder and president of Monroe Petroleum."

I studied them as the car drove slowly past the stands. George appeared to be in his fifties, with a rugged, handsome face under his cowboy hat. Faye was much younger, her ash-blonde hair styled in a flip with bangs wisping her small-boned face. Her smile radiated a white-toothed brilliance. She wore a pageant sash across a glittery jacket.

"Next please welcome this year's Miss Rodeo North Dakota 1966, Miss Sandra Collins, and her court, Miss . . ."

The crowd cheered and clapped as the names washed over me. The pickup trucks with the pageant winners standing in the beds paraded slowly in front of the crowd. The women waved gloved hands and flashed toothy grins beneath white cowgirl hats. Wolf whistles rang out.

An uncomfortable feeling of discomfiture settled over me. North Dakota seemed out of step with the rest of the country. I compared the scene in front of me to the national headlines in the newspaper. Elsewhere, young women donned their hip-huggers while marching for equal rights. Men burned their draft cards protesting their involuntary shipment to the jungles of South Vietnam. Black people marched with Martin Luther King Jr. The country was changing, the establishment being torn down and a new age ushered in.

But here, women paraded in beauty queen regalia and men showed off their chaps and spurs. Even the music was out of step. Instead of rocking to the Rolling Stones and the Beatles, the ever-present polka music blared from the speakers.

It was 1966, wasn't it? Where did I fit into this changing status quo?

A ragtag band rode in the bed of the last pickup truck, trumpeting and drumming a marching tune. They arrived at what served as the grandstand.

"Please stand for the national anthem!"

The polka music screeched to a halt as we stood dutifully. The band attempted the opening chords. "Oh, say, can you see . . ." the crowd warbled.

Our attention was drawn to the central ring, surrounded by recently constructed fencing. Inside was a wide patch of dirt and sawdust. At the far end, gates held animals in slotted corrals. Two rodeo clowns entered the ring, waving to the crowd.

The rodeo began as a wooden gate swung open and a rider on horseback burst through the chute like a firecracker. Gripping the reins in one hand, the cowboy flung his other arm up in the air. The bronco arched its backbone, bucking its back legs in a frantic series of spasmatic kicks. The crowd bellowed as the rider crashed to the ground, rolling out of the way of the pounding hooves.

I leaned over to Frank. "Why does the horse buck like that?"

"They put a strap on it. Around its abdomen. See?" he pointed at the beast.

At that moment, George and Faye appeared, making their way along the foot of the bleachers. Frank raised his hand and waved. George acknowledged him and conferred with his wife, and they climbed the steps toward us.

"Howdy, Frank," George said, extending a handshake down the riser. "This is my wife, Faye."

"Nice to meet you, Faye." Frank nodded to her. "This is my better half, Henrietta."

I greeted them. George looked me over. Faye shared a smile that reached her eyes. We scooted over, and they settled next to us on the bleachers.

George leaned across Frank. "How're you enjoyin' North Dakota, Henrietta?" he asked.

"Well, it sure is different," I said.

I felt Frank stiffen beside me.

"Different than the East Coast, I mean," I fumbled. "I mean, the weather. It's just as hot but drier."

George laughed. "Yeah, I'll bet."

A cheer rang out as the chute opened again, and another rider dressed all in black shot out of the gate. The bronco leaped and kicked as if in agony. Mere seconds later the rider was tossed to the ground, dust billowing around him. He cocooned in the dust and rolled out of the way of stomping hooves just in the nick of time. One of the rodeo clowns waved his arms to distract the horse.

"Isn't that dangerous?" I asked.

George nodded. "Oh yeah, but the cowboys practice. They know the risks. Rodeo's a lifestyle for 'em."

I paused for a moment. "I meant dangerous for the horse."

Frank's eyes narrowed and he pursed his lips. George cleared his throat, speechless.

Spectators milled around at the base of the stands. The bleachers shook like ocean waves as people clambered up and down.

"Will ya look at that," George said, his voice lowered. He half nodded toward the crowd below. A group of men in traditional native dress stood to one side. Feathers adorned their black hair. "What are they thinkin' comin' here dressed like that?"

"Are they American Indians?" I asked.

"Yeah, probably outta Fort Berthold," George replied.

"Aren't they allowed to be here?" I asked. Frank elbowed me in the side. I raised my eyes toward him and squinted. Had I said something wrong?

George growled, "They're just tryin' to stir up trouble dressed like that. There's a whole native movement startin'. They want all of the land to be declared as theirs. They're tryin' to stop the drillin' in North Dakota and Montana, claimin' the land was stolen from them years ago. They say it's sacred."

"They think the land itself is sacred?" I asked. Frank cleared his throat.

George replied, "Everythin' is sacred to 'em. Even trees and rocks. Can you imagine? Ridiculous."

"*Was* the land taken from them?"

He rubbed his hand over his face. "The treaties were agreed to long ago. It's way too late to go back now."

I stared down at the group of men. They stood, arms crossed, faces set. The crowd swerved around them, avoiding them like a nest of scorpions. If they were protesting against age-old treaties, it wasn't apparent, at least to me.

The day wore on, the sun lifting higher as the earth spun on its axis. A veil of cirrus clouds streaked the sky like raw cotton. I swatted at a buzzing horsefly near my ear. Faye spent the time descending and ascending the bleachers like a tiny sprite on a mission. She seemed to know everyone there. She was either calling out to folks and waving or rushing down to greet them, hugging and smiling.

"Faye sure knows a lot of people," I said to George.

He chuckled. "That woman could talk the ear off a stalk of corn. Did you know she writes the social column for the *Dickerson Press*? She knows everythin' about everybody."

Around noon, Frank and George climbed down to buy us lunch. Faye scooched over to sit next to me. We watched as cowgirls rode horses around a set of barrels. Dirt exploded around the horses' hooves as the riders leaned into the turns. The riders whooped, colorful plaid shirts rippling, feet dug into stirrups, hats bouncing on their heads.

"Do you have any children, Henrietta?" Faye asked. This seemed like an odd question because if I did, where would they be other than here?

"Oh, God, no," I said, my hand to my chest. Her eyes widened. "I mean, Frank and I just got married in June."

She nodded. "Oh, that's right. George did say something like that. What've you been doing since you moved here? Do you go to church?"

I shook my head. "No. I don't think there's a church in Mammoth."

"No, there isn't. You'd have to go into Dickerson."

"Um, no. We haven't done that." I looked at her face. "*Yet*, I mean."

"What's kept you busy so far?"

I shrugged. "We've done some hiking in the badlands. And Frank took me to see one of his oil rigs."

"He did? Well, you don't hear that every day. What do you plan to do this winter? Once the weather sets in? Do you sew? Or knit or quilt, anything like that?"

I scrunched my forehead. "No."

"Do you play bridge?"

"No, I've never learned."

"How about cooking? Do you like to cook or bake?"

"Not really. I'm a paleontologist. I guess what I like to do is dig up stuff. And study fossils."

She stared at me with wide eyes. "Oh."

I was paddling against the current here. A moment later someone called up to Faye. She waved back, excused herself, and climbed down the bleachers. I exhaled a sigh of relief at her retreat.

The men returned. Frank handed me a hamburger. "The guy said this is the best burger west of the Mississippi." I unwrapped the paper wrapper and stared at the ground meat inside. Grease escaped and ran down my hand.

"Next up! Calf roping!" boomed the announcer, the words traveling across the stands.

A frantic calf ran out of a gate, flanked by a horseman. Twirling a lasso overhead, the cowboy dipped the rope, looping and tightening it around the calf's neck. In a fluid motion, the rider leaped off his horse, sprinted to the calf, picked up the poor creature, and slammed it down on its side. The crowd cheered as its legs were trussed together like a Thanksgiving turkey. It emitted a sad, bleating sound.

I stared at the hamburger in my hand, rewrapped it, and set it down on the bleacher. I looked at Frank. "I think I'm going to buy some popcorn."

The afternoon began to morph into evening, the shadows lengthening. The crowd thinned, and pickups escaped down the highway in both directions. Frank and I crossed at the post office and headed for home.

"Henrietta, you do understand that when someone asks you a question, you can tell them what they might want to hear, right? It doesn't have to be true."

I looked over at him. "What do you mean?"

"Like when George asked you if you like it here in North Dakota? You could just have said yes. That you like it."

I stared at him, squinting, the setting sun on my face. The corners of my mouth turned down. "But I don't know if I like it yet. We've only been here a few months."

"That's beside the point. He'll want to hear that you like it here. That way he doesn't have to worry that I'll want to quit and move away."

"So I should lie?"

Frank ran his hand over his face. "What did you and Faye talk about?"

"All the things she thought I might be interested in. None of which I am."

Frank let out a small sigh, his mouth set in a line. We walked on. I felt I had somehow failed an exam for which there had been no material available to study.

Dickerson Press, September 15, 1966
Western Whispers
by Faye Monroe

*Bronco busters, calf ropers, and trick riders mes-
merized the crowd on Saturday at the spectacular
Mammoth Rodeo. Sunny weather blessed the crowd
as they enjoyed all the afternoon had to offer. The children especially loved the antics of the rodeo clowns.*

*The royal rodeo court sparkled like diamonds
at their crowning by Mr. George Monroe, this year's
master of ceremonies. Miss Rodeo 1966, Miss Sandra
Collins, wore the tiara proudly with her lovely smile
and shimmering ensemble. The processional parade
included the Veterans of Foreign Wars presenting
the Stars and Stripes. Tunes were supplied by the
Dickerson High School alumni band.*

*A good time was had by all, although one newly
arrived East Coaster was heard to say she was concerned for the rodeo animals. Welcome to the West,
honey! . . .*

As I read Faye's social column in the newspaper, every nerve in
my body screamed for me to crawl back into bed, enshroud myself
in blankets, and never emerge, like a caterpillar in a perpetual chrysalis. The only saving grace was she did not mention me by name.
Of course, how many "newly arrived East Coasters" could there be?

———◆———

I pored over the chapter on the High Plains in my shabby copy of
Botany of the Western States. Mammoth was situated in the mixed-
grass prairie region, between the Rocky Mountain rain shadow to
the west and deposits from the last continental glaciers to the east.

Grasses here were both short and tall. Buffalo grass and blue grama. Indian grass and switchgrass. Little bluestem and wheatgrass and needlegrass. What was needleleaf sedge? I resisted the urge to throw up my hands in surrender as I sat on our sofa studying the hand-drawn sketches of each species. The front door banged open and Frank stomped inside.

I looked up to find his face a mountain of thunder. He tossed his briefcase like an Olympic shot putter, and it clanged down onto the coffee table in front of me.

"What on earth is the matter?" I asked, shutting my book and rising off the couch. "Bad day?"

"Yeah, you might say that," he said, his arms folded. "At the rodeo, did you tell Faye that I had taken you to the rig?"

I took a moment before replying. "Oh, yes, I guess I did . . ."

"Why the hell did you do that? Didn't I tell you that it might not be allowed?" He crossed to stand in front of me. His face started to turn a slight shade of purple.

"No one stopped us once I was there," I said, my voice catching. "I didn't know it was a big secret after I was allowed in the trailer."

Frank shook his head, seething, his eyes hard. "Henrietta, use your common sense. I never told anyone at the office that I took you. Technically, everything we do at work is confidential. How many times do I have to tell you that?"

Tears threatened, and I blinked them back. "Maybe you shouldn't have taken me. It was all for nothing anyway."

"Honestly, right now, I think you might be right. I was trying to help you with your job interview, and now it's backfired. I must have lost my mind."

"Are you in a lot of trouble?"

"George isn't happy, I'll tell you that. He pulled me into his office and reamed me a new one. Now I've got a warning on my record."

I gulped, a thick knot in my throat. "I'm so sorry, Frank. I guess I just didn't think. Faye was asking me all these questions, one after another, and I just blurted it out."

He shook his head. "Well, next time think twice before blurting the first thing that comes into your head. The last person you want to tell your business to is a newspaper reporter, for God's sake. Especially one who happens to be married to my boss."

Frank stormed past me, entered our bedroom, and slammed the door shut. As I listened to its angry reverberation, a tear trickled down my cheek. I brushed it away with the back of my hand. I had messed up by blathering to Faye. Making casual conversation had never been my forte. Words launched from my tongue without my brain's consent. Grabbing the newspaper, I stuffed it underneath the couch. No reason for Frank to see Faye's column. That would be like pouring water on a grease fire.

I stared out the front window at the patchy grass clumps. At that moment my marriage seemed as weedy as our overgrown lawn.

CHAPTER 9

October brought a bite to the morning air as if Jack Frost hid just around the corner, smirking and biding his time. My morning meanderings widened in area as I explored the dirt roads and byways around town. Most of the lanes ended at farmhouses, with fallow fields stretching in all directions like rectangular earthen pieces of a giant patchwork quilt. Ringing the fields, trees donned their autumn hues, the amber of the cottonwoods (*Populus deltoides*), brilliant yellows of the green ash (*Fraxinus pennsylvanica*), and the dull yellows of the box elder (*Acer negundo*—a species of maple) standing in sharp contrast against the conifers. The eastern red cedars (*Juniperus virginiana*) had transformed in color from their summer dark green into autumnal reddish brown.

From the scientific names, I deduced the trees were native elsewhere, and some research confirmed this hypothesis. The trees in Mammoth had been planted in a conservation effort during the 1930s and 1940s. They formed shelter belts, which were windbreaks to prevent erosion. The trees grew in rows—usually five to seven—each extending about a half mile in length. Their position depended on the field to be protected, some oriented north-south, others east-west.

The rows alternated with a mixture of trees. Several rows were planted with only conifers. Since conifers did not lose their leaves in winter, they provided yearlong protection against the wind. The pines and junipers were interspersed with the now golden-leafed hardwoods. Around the trunks, an understory of Tartarian hon-eysuckle, common lilac, and chokecherry grew in a dense thicket. A cacophony of leaves swayed in the gentle breeze, and I pulled my jacket tighter around my throat. I realized I should head back home, so I turned and crossed a strip of meadow. Late-blooming prairie coneflowers bent their droopy heads in the wind, and curly-cup gumweed stuck to my socks as I plowed through. I reached a dirt lane and strode toward town. The cloudless cobalt sky rounded above me. With the sun reddening my face, I took in the view as I walked. The flat topography of the land stretched in all directions, monotonous yet strangely peaceful. My revelry was broken by a persistent buzzing, and I looked down at my feet. A yellow jacket landed on my leg and I let out a cry, jumping aside and brushing it off. Wasps buzzed, swarming around an entrance hole in the ground. My heartbeat accelerated as I scampered away, my tennis shoes kick-ing up dust in my wake.

I slowed as I passed Janine's house, which looked deserted. When I thought about it, I realized she had been out of sight for several days, which was unusual. Almost daily, I would see her in her back-yard, hanging out laundry on a clothesline, with clothespins between her lips. She owned a metal basket contraption with a liner to hold the clothes, and she would often wave to me as she wheeled it across the bumpy ground. From my side window, I could view the para-phernalia of her young family's life—sheets, underwear, socks, girl's smocked dresses, boy's plaid shirts. Usually, the twins were outside with her, tossing a ball or digging in their sandbox. But not today.

The front door to her home opened and Janine stepped out. I sensed immediately that something was wrong. She wore a wrinkled shirt over her jeans, and her shoulder-length blonde hair looked uncombed. Worry lines stretched across her forehead.

"Henrietta. Can you come here, please? I need your help," she called.

I hastened to her door. As I approached I noticed the dark circles beneath her eyes.

"Of course. What's the matter, Janine?"

"It's Michael," she said. "He's got a fever, and I need to take him to a doctor."

She opened the door wider, and I stepped inside. The shades were lowered, casting dark shadows over her living room. Her furniture did indeed look like mine, but even more dilapidated, lending a note of despair to the stuffy room. I looked toward the back of the house, through the opening to the kitchen. Diane sat at a table, staring unseeingly with puffy eyes into a bowl of cornflakes.

"Do you think he has the flu?" I asked.

"No," Janine said, shaking her head. "Nothing like that. He scratched his leg a few days ago on the metal edge of the sandbox. I put some witch hazel on it and didn't think anything more about it. The cut didn't seem too deep. But yesterday he spiked a fever, so I gave him some baby aspirin. And now the cut is inflamed and oozy, and his fever is higher. I'm worried his leg is infected."

"It sounds like it might be," I said. "Do you have a car? I didn't see one outside."

"No. John took it with him to the rig. He's not due back for another four days. I called Ada, and she said she could take us to Dickerson. She's closing the post office. I was going to take Diane with us, but since you're here, do you think you could stay and watch her?"

Diane's head popped up from her bowl and she looked at me, her face equally alarmed and suspicious.

I stifled my initial response of terror and said, "Of course."

A groan emitted from a room on the left, and Janine turned and hurried into what I assumed was Michael's bedroom. At the same time, a knock sounded at the front door and it cracked open. Ada stuck her head inside, her eyes holding a worried look.

"Oh, hello, Henrietta." She stepped inside and lowered her voice. "Janine must be really concerned about Michael. She sounded panicked on the phone, which isn't like her."

I replied, "She thinks he has an infected leg. She's in there with him now." I pointed toward the bedroom.

Ada crossed the living room, her cowboy boots clomping over the linoleum floor. "How's the patient?" she called ahead as she disappeared into the room. I walked to the kitchen at the back of the house. Dirty dishes rested in the sink. Diane perched on her chair, her feet not reaching the ground. Cornflakes, untouched, wilted soggily in her bowl.

"Hi, Diane. Aren't you hungry?" I asked.

Her lower lip quivered. "Michael's sick," she whispered, dropping her spoon on the table with a clang.

"I know. But your mom's going to take him to the doctor, and he'll make him better. That's what doctors do, right?"

"I don't like the doctor. He gives me shots."

"Yeah, nobody likes shots," I said. "Is it all right if I stay here with you while Michael and your mom go to the doctor?"

Her eyes teared at that. "I guess so," she said in her tiny voice.

"Don't worry. We'll have fun," I said. "Maybe we can make a get-well card for Michael?"

"Okay."

I turned at the sound of voices. Janine crossed the living room with Michael in her arms. His head hung to one side, pale and listless. Ada rushed ahead to hold open the front door.

"Diane, be a good girl for Mrs. Bailey," Janine called out. "We'll be back soon, I promise."

"Soon" was a time term, and to a five-year-old, "soon" might be an hour. A whole morning was an age. A day was an epoch. Overnight was a geological period. By the next afternoon, an era of time would pass for Diane, crawling by in sluggish footsteps, a clock in slow motion.

I had no idea what to do with a five-year-old. First, we located construction paper and crayons and made a card for Michael. Diane drew a picture of Michael on it, with his leg dripping red blood.

She printed her name on the inside, and I wrote "Get Well Soon," although I was unsure why, since I did not know if he could read. I cleaned up the dishes, with Diane attempting to help. At lunchtime, I unwrapped limp American cheese slices, grilled two sandwiches, and coaxed Diane to eat some of hers. The specter of a long afternoon loomed in front of us. I did not want to leave the house and miss a phone call, so playing in the yard was out. This proved not to be an issue, as Diane was now spooked by the sandbox and wanted to stay inside.

"Want to see my Barbies?" she asked.

"Sure." I followed her into the bedroom. Diane and Michael shared the room. Two twin beds lined opposite walls, both unmade. I walked over to the far one and pulled up the sheets and a navy-blue quilt. A poster from the television show *Voyage to the Bottom of the Sea* hung over Michael's bed. Diane saw me staring at it.

"That's Michael's," she said. "He wants to be like Kowalski and live in a submarine."

"Ah," I said, looking up at the Barbie poster above her bed. The blonde-haired, blue-eyed seductress stared back at me through cat-eye glasses. "And what do you want to be when you grow up?" I asked.

Diane reached down and picked up a Barbie doll from her floor. I girded myself for her response.

"I'm going to be an astronaut," she said.

My eyes widened. I failed to hide the shock on my face. "An astronaut? Far out! What an exciting job that will be."

She nodded, her soulful eyes looking up at me. "I'm going to travel on a spaceship to the moon. Like Barbie." She held the Barbie up to show me. Sure enough, the doll was dressed in a silver flight suit, with a white helmet and zippered boots.

We settled on the braided throw rug on her floor. "What other outfits does Barbie have?" I asked.

I was surprised to find that Barbie had quite a varied set of costumes. Diane owned two of the fashion dolls. The second doll modeled a blue gown with a white fur collar and long white gloves, ready for any formal occasion. Barbie could ice-skate with her metallic skates, a pink leotard and skirt, and fleecy white mittens. In case she was invited to tea, she could don a pink chiffon jumpsuit and pour from a silver teapot. She could prepare dinner with her *Barbie's Easy-As-Pie Cookbook* and her pots and pans while wearing a dotted housedress. Her gold-striped gown and white high heels would be perfect for a dance. Closer to my heart, her red houndstooth "teacher dress" came with a globe and geography book.

It seemed that Barbie had a far better wardrobe and social life than I ever would.

Janine's voice on the telephone came across the line heavy with exhaustion, as if every word took a herculean effort.

"Henrietta? I'm at the hospital. The doctor took one look at Michael's leg and sent us to the emergency room. They admitted him right away."

"How's he doing?"

She began to sniffle. "He has an infection in his leg. And he's just lying there in bed. I'm not sure he knows what's going on or where he is."

I swallowed a lump forming in my throat. "I'm so sorry, Janine. But he'll be fine, I'm sure."

"His fever's still one hundred and two. They're trying to bring it down."

"Were you able to get ahold of John at the rig?"

She heaved a ragged sigh. "Yes, finally. He's on his way, but the rig's near Casper, so it'll be a while."

Diane's head popped out of her bedroom doorway. "Is that Mommy?"

I nodded at her and motioned for her to come toward me.

"Diane wants to say hello. Is that all right?" I asked into the phone.

"Just a minute." I heard Janine blow her nose. "Yes. Is everything going okay there?"

"Oh yes, we're absolutely fine. Don't worry about a thing. We've been playing with Barbies in her room. And I can spend the night." Diane looked up at me, her face more anguished than any five-year-old's should ever be. I handed the receiver to her.

"Mommy?" she said into the telephone, her voice shaking.

Right then my heart broke a little for her, a child at the end of a line, left with someone she barely knew.

Later, after a dinner of Chicken and Stars soup and saltine crackers, I turned on their black-and-white television and wiggled the rabbit ears, trying to get reception. We did not own a TV, so watching a show was somewhat of a treat for me. Diane and I scrunched on the couch together in our pajamas—Frank had brought mine over earlier. Stripes, a battered old tabby cat, settled on the end of the couch and glared at me with yellow-slitted eyes. The show *Daktari* came on, and Diane laughed at Clarence, the cross-eyed lion, and Judy the chimp as Dr. Tracy saved a giraffe from a poacher's bullet.

"I think it's time for bed," I announced once the program was over, standing up and switching off the set.

"But I'm not tired," Diane said, rubbing her eyes.

"How about we get your teeth brushed anyway?"

"Okay." I followed her into the bathroom.

"Do you need help?" I asked.

"Maybe with the toothpaste."

After I helped her wash her face and brush her teeth, she looked up at me. "I don't want to go to bed."

"Why not?"

"Because Michael isn't here," she said.

My heart softened at her sad expression. "Well, maybe we can just stretch out on your bed and read a book?" I asked. "Do you have a favorite book?"

She nodded.

"Let's go find it, okay?"

She led me to her bedroom and pointed to the closet. "My books are in there."

I peeked inside. A stack of children's books rested on a low shelf. "Which one is your favorite?"

She reached inside and, one by one, examined each book, picking it up and then setting it aside. Geologic time was faster than this, I thought.

"This one," she said finally.

"*Fox in Socks.* Oh, I like Dr. Seuss too," I said.

Diane climbed into bed and leaned against her pillow. I reclined next to her.

"Fox, socks, box, knox . . ." I began, reading with a hushed, rhythmic cadence. By the time I reached "Hose goes, Rose grows," Diane's breathing had shallowed. I glanced over, noting her closed, translucent eyelids fluttering in sleep.

Observing her sweet face, angelic in slumber, I reviewed the day in my mind. Perhaps this was what parenthood would be like. A pendulum swinging between joy and terror. Oscillating between adoration and frustration. Shooting for the moon and plunging into the hadal abyss. The zenith and the nadir of life. Would I ever be ready for that?

CHAPTER 10

After four days, Janine brought Michael home, his fever vanquished and his leg swollen but healing. Ada and I had traded off with babysitting Diane. By then I had been exposed to both *Star Trek*, with that handsome Captain Kirk, and *Batman*—Pow! Wham! Socko! My time with the five-year-old had been eye-opening. That said, once Janine returned, she gathered her brood like a hen with her chicks and ushered me out the door with a profusion of rushed thanks.

The specter of winter now rested on my shoulders. Like a bear approaching hibernation, I prepared for the seclusion of the months ahead. In town, the few aspen trees (*Populus tremuloides*), bereft of their leaves, joined the blackjack pines (*Pinus ponderosa*) in a groaning cacophony against the increasing wind. Deciding to load up on books, I scurried along the sidewalk, grocery bag in hand.

Gusts pressed against the bookshop's door as I hefted it open, sliding inside. The door slammed shut behind me, trapping the scent of cigarette smoke that lingered in the air. The interior appeared vacant. On the desk perched a handwritten sign: "Honor system— leave money here."

"Hello!" I called. "Kima?"

No answer, which did not seem all that unusual. Who was I to understand the machinations of her mind?

The stacks beckoned me, and my eyes swooped up and down the spines. I pulled books from the metal shelves, examined the covers, read the synopses, and decided pro or con. My grocery bag, propped open at my feet, filled with my selections. John le Carré, Agatha Christie, Kurt Vonnegut, and James Michener settled on the top, ready to engage my mind in the weeks ahead.

Finished, I tried again. "Kima, are you here?"

She did not appear from the back room on her strangely silent feet. I dug into my change purse, counted out the coins, and set them on the desk. My arms burdened with my stuffed bag, I leaned my shoulder into the door and exited the shop.

The breeze chapped my cheeks and pushed me along the sidewalk as the cold air slid through my knitted mittens like prickly serpent teeth. I neared the highway as a wrinkled man with a wide, gray mustache careened out of the bank and walked toward me.

"Morning," he said. "Did you find all the books you wanted?" He dipped his battered cowboy hat as he nodded toward my bag.

"Yep," I answered. "All set for winter."

He coughed as he laughed, a raspy fluid sound. "You might need even more than that to make it through all the snow." He rambled on past me.

I glanced down at my pile of books as I met the deserted highway. Reading had always been my escape. I hoped these stories would be enough to entertain me for a while. Who knew when Kima would open the store next? Certainly not me.

I purchased my stockpile of books just in time. Winter slammed down like a howling child, angry at being ignored. The jet stream swung south from Saskatchewan, and Arctic air sank with negative buoyancy, bringing frigid temperatures. Then the air pressure lessened as winds rushed to fill cyclones churning counterclockwise with Coriolis force. Bitter snow bludgeoned down along cold fronts. I hunkered inside our house, the wind buffeting the siding and beating on the window glass. The cottonwood tree in our yard bent like an old crone. Frank drove away each day, either to his office in Dickerson or out to the oil fields, in our only mode of transportation other than our feet. I was left to fend for myself in the sparely furnished rooms.

Almost six months had passed since my graduation, and not using my education gnawed at my core. I worried I was becoming like my mother, resentful and restless. Determined to avoid that fate, I tried to stay busy. I cleaned the house, then cleaned it again. I washed our clothes and hung them to dry on clotheslines in the bathroom. I pulled out my Betty Crocker cookbook and unboxed a dutch oven we had received as a wedding gift. I managed to stew a chicken and create vegetable noodle soup and repeated those recipes over and over. All this turned into a self-perpetuating prophecy, as I saw myself digging the same trench my mother occupied. That of homemaker. The very last thing I wanted to become.

I distracted myself by reading my books. Mysteries, westerns, science fiction, history, and science, all gleaned from Kima's store. After years of specializing, I was now a generalist. Freed from scientific papers on paleobotany, I absorbed stories and facts from other places—crossing the desert in Afghanistan, diving in the Azores, paddling up the Amazon. I was a spy, a heroine, a space traveler, a jilted princess who had the last word.

Yet still, an unrequited longing to do more, to study, to make a difference in my field, interrupted my revelry like a monster from within.

At night, Frank and I made love on our lumpy double mattress, in church-approved matrimony, with the Commonwealth of Virginia seal stamped on our license stored away in a box. And in the mornings, I swallowed that liberating of all inventions—the Pill.

The snow continued, falling in sheeted torrents, sticking to the shelter belts and filling the ditches with gritty graupel. Frost grew fernlike across our single-paned windows, the glass groaning in icy agony. Our power flickered, vanished, and then reappeared like a genie. The furnace crackled and the radiators thunked. On the coldest mornings, I could see my breath inside the house.

Occasionally I observed Janine outside with Diane and Michael. While she shoveled the driveway, the children tumbled in the snow, like padded acrobats. Michael's leg had healed, and he seemed back to his normal self, at least from my vantage point down the street. I waved from my doorstep, and they waved back, but other than a few quick visits for cups of coffee, our contact was minimal.

After two months inside with no end in sight, I felt like an animal wanting to claw its way out. I wrote letters to my mother. To my Aunt Esther. To Delilah. How many ways could I describe the roaring of the wind?

Dear Mother,
   The North Dakota winter has arrived. The wind
howls continually like a predatory wolf . . .

Dear Aunt Esther,
   The North Dakota winter has arrived. The wind
screeches like a possessed banshee . . .

Hello Delilah,
   The North Dakota winter has arrived. The wind
rages like a yowling asylum inmate . . .

I was running out of similes. I stamped the envelopes and donned my outdoor winter ensemble. Layers of shirts, tights under pants, long socks under my field boots, wool coat, hat, and mittens. I set out, walking like an Inuit stalking a walrus, carefully placing each footfall along the vacant, ice-covered streets. Stratocumulus clouds rolled overhead with a patina of tarnished silver. The air chapped my cheeks and tore the breath from my lungs.

The tiny brick post office on Main Street looked like a frosted elf's bungalow. I passed the frozen blue letterbox and pushed open the door. Ada hunched in front of a space heater while sorting the mail. A microburst of frigid air surged with me through the open door.

"Hidey-ho!" she beckoned to me. "Hurry up and close that door."

"Sorry," I said, pressing the door closed behind me, shutting out the polar blast. "I wanted to mail these and figured I needed the exercise." I slid the letters toward her.

"How ya doin' in this weather?" she asked. "I haven't seen much of you."

I took a big breath and let it out slowly. "I'm going stir-crazy, to tell you the truth."

She nodded and picked up my envelopes, tapping them on the counter. "Oh, yeah, it's that time of year. Snowflakes as big as birds. Do you get into Dickerson at all? There's more to do there. A bowling alley, movie theater, shops."

"We go twice a month for groceries. Frank takes the car to work every day. If I'd go with him to town, I'd have to stay the whole day until five o'clock."

"Small towns aren't for everybody," Ada said as she reached behind her and pulled some envelopes from a cubbyhole. "Here's your mail. Looks like you have a letter. And, ooh, an invitation to the Monroe's Christmas party."

Did she know everyone's business?

I grabbed the offered letters and stuck them in my coat pocket. "George Monroe is Frank's boss," I said.

"Hoity-toity," she replied.

Once home and freed from my layers and boots, I reclined on the couch and tore open a letter from Delilah. News from home fed my soul like manna to the starving Israelites. I recognized her hasty scrawl.

> *Hello Henrietta,*
> *I finally have a chance to sit down and write.*
> *Kelvin and I have been terribly busy with the anti-war*

effort. Early this month we traveled to Harvard University to join the students there in protest. It was a glorious day, all of us demonstrating in common purpose in Harvard Yard. I can't describe the sense of camaraderie we felt with the crowd (although most were men, of course). We stopped that warmonger, Robert McNamara, from leaving campus without addressing our concerns. He was shoved up onto a car hood and made to answer questions about the war. In the end, the police had to escort him off campus.

In January we're planning to go to New York City. A group of artists are organizing a protest there. We'll keep going until this senseless war ends. I feel like I've woken up and am finally making a difference in this world. I hope you are finding your place in it also.

With peace and love to you and Frank,
Delilah

I leaned back and closed my eyes. If I felt purposeless before, I was now an empty husk, drained of meaning. Delilah had always been a rebel, my outgoing, cigarette-smoking, tequila-drinking roommate. Yet now I hardly recognized her as she pushed for justice in a war-torn world. Passions flamed across America. Students demonstrated against the war on college campuses. American Indian activists protested police brutality. Martin Luther King marched in Chicago. And women picketed for equal rights. The times were simultaneously intoxicating and terrifying. And here I was, inside a self-constructed, frozen bubble.

When would I do something significant with my life?

CHAPTER 11

The faded garment bag hung in the back of my closet like an artifact long ago discovered and subsequently forgotten. It housed
a relic from my past, an emerald-green evening gown with crinoline
underskirts. Probably out of fashion, but the closest thing I owned
for a semiformal Christmas party. I unzipped the bag and inhaled
the slightly musty scent.

Frank looked over from knotting his tie. *Why did men always get
to wear the same thing—pants, jacket, tie—but women had to come
up with different outfits for every party? Not that I went to parties, but
it seemed unfair nonetheless.*

"Where did you get that dress?" Frank asked.

"College," I replied. I stepped my nylon-clad legs into the dress
and pulled it up around me. "Zip?"

"I know a cocktail party isn't your favorite vibe," Frank said as
he pulled up the zipper along the back of my dress. "But all the geologists who work for George have been invited. You'll get to meet
their wives. Remember to tell everyone how much you love living
in North Dakota."

"Yeah, I know. Don't worry. I can lie and tell them how much I
love it here. I'll try not to embarrass you." I twirled in front of the
mirror, my mind changing my reflection into that of a younger me,
headed to her first dance. A college boy—what had been his name
again?—had invited me. I remembered the ballroom at the Campus

Center, decorated with streamers, dancing to Elvis Presley, and receiving my first kiss out on the balcony. Right before Mr. Prince Charming graduated and disappeared into the ether.

"You look beautiful in that dress," Frank said, his eyes softening.

"And I didn't mean that you'd embarrass me."

"Oh, just wait until I have a few whiskey sours in me," I said, winking at him. "Then all bets are off."

───◆───

Gales blew glistening flurries of snow across our headlights. An iridescent cloud halo surrounded a first-quarter moon, giving little illumination to the back roads. George and Faye lived on the outskirts of Dickerson, in what was described as a "ranch house." Frank squinted through the windshield, both hands gripping the steering wheel, while I read the directions and watched for landmarks.

"'Drive two miles down the gravel road. Then turn left at the entrance.'"

A matching set of stone pillars flanking an open wrought-iron gate appeared through the gloom. I pointed at it.

"There it is."

We turned and drove down a long driveway, approaching the house. A magnificent log cabin came into view, gleaming in outdoor spotlights. Along the front, a two-story wall of glass windows revealed an immense Christmas tree inside, glittering with white lights. Broad outdoor decks lined two side wings. A river-rocked chimney towered from the multipeaked, snow-laden roof.

We pulled to a stop and stared, mouths ajar.

"Oh my God," I said. "I guess being president of your own oil company pays well. Or owning cattle does."

Frank gave a short laugh. "Oh yeah. Not to mention George owns the mineral rights under all his properties. Rumor is he studied petroleum engineering so he would understand how to drill for oil under his land."

"Lucky him," I said.

We parked in a side pasture next to a line of cars. My feet froze instantly in my ballet flats as we rushed across the crust of snow to the front door. Under my coat, my outfit of gauze, netting, and nylon did nothing to keep me warm.

The door opened before we had a chance to knock.

"Welcome, please come in!" George stood in the foyer, dressed in a smart gray suit and cowboy boots. "Frank, Henrietta, great to see you. Thanks for comin'. The girl will check your coat." As if on cue, a young woman stepped forward, taking our coats.

"Thank you for the invitation," Frank said.

A large wooden display case stretched along the back of the entry foyer. Glass shelves held a collection of Indian artifacts. I meandered over.

"Wow, look at all these arrowheads. And spearpoints," I said. "I wonder how old they are?"

George followed us. "Those were all found on my land," he said, waving his hand across the shelves. "This Indian stuff doesn't appeal to me, but Faye just loves to collect it."

I gazed at the display. The arrowheads presented a myriad of hues—white, ocher, russet, gray, black—probably varieties of quartz and flint. I itched to touch them. Pieces of broken pottery were sprinkled like breadcrumbs on the bottom shelf. In the neighboring cabinet, a pair of moccasins shone under a light, the tiny bright-colored beads so delicate I could not imagine threading them. Next to them sat a quilled bag with intricate geometric designs. Most impressive was a large wooden mask with a birdlike beak. I pointed at it, my finger resting on the case's glass.

"I wonder if that was used in ceremonies?" I asked, but George's attention was diverted to other guests pushing through the door behind us.

Frank put his hand on my back and propelled me toward the grand living room. "Let's move on," he whispered in my ear.

I gaped like a lunatic as we entered the living room.

A fire blazed in the enormous stone fireplace, lending a smoky essence to the room. The shaggy head of a buffalo hung above the hearth, its black glass eyes glaring at the guests. Hand-carved wooden figurines of wild animals—deer, bears, wolves—decorated the holly-draped mantle. Overhead, elk antlers ringed a glowing chandelier. Buttery leather couches and chairs formed seating groups, with end tables displaying sparkling geodes—polished slabs of amethyst, citrine, and smoky and milky quartz on pedestals. Cocktail tables perched in corners, hosting plates filled with cheeses and nuts. On the far side of the room, a bartender poured drinks behind a knotty pine bar. Guests mingled in clumps, displaying their finery while drinking the proffered alcohol. Bing Crosby crooned "White Christmas" from a hidden stereo.

We crossed to the lofty Christmas tree, drawn by the glow of hundreds of pearly lights. I whiffed its piney scent. It certainly was not anything like the reused metallic tree of my youth.

"Where do you think they got that tree?" I whispered to Frank.

"They probably brought it in from out of state. Maybe Minnesota."

"That must have cost a pretty penny."

Steering around several groups of guests, we headed to the bar. "Beer, please," Frank said to the bartender. He turned to me. "What do you want to drink?"

"A whiskey sour?" I asked. My mother's old standby.

"A whiskey sour for my wife," Frank parroted to the bartender like he was Lieutenant Uhura on *Star Trek*.

"Recognize anyone?" I asked as our drinks slid toward us.

"A few. Come on, I'll introduce you."

I gulped my whiskey sour for bravery and we tossed ourselves into the fray. Conversations buzzed and hummed around us. I was introduced to Frank's coworkers and their wives. Halfway through my whiskey sour, I had no hope of remembering anyone's name the next day.

There was no doubt the minute Faye Monroe swept in. She commanded the room in her scarlet, cleavage-revealing gown. Her blonde hair was styled in an upsweep, and diamond pendants dangled from her ears and sparkled around her throat. The seas seemed to part for her as her voice carried across the expanse. She nodded and greeted the groups of guests as she made her way to the middle of the room.

George joined her, gazing at her with an adoring face as if he had just won the lottery. They stopped in front of the fireplace. The volume of the music decreased by some unseen hand, and the crowd hushed.

Faye began, "How wonderful to see everyone, family and friends. Welcome to our home. We're so excited to have you here to celebrate Christmas with us."

George shared a smile and held up a glass. "Thank you, all, for coming. Merry Christmas, everyone! Cheers!"

We all raised our glasses and answered the toast. At that cue, folding doors were pushed aside accordion-style by waitstaff to reveal the dining room. Buffet tables rimmed the room, heaped with overflowing platters.

"Dinner is served. Enjoy!" George announced.

The music resumed and the party swung back into rhythm. I was feeling somewhat tipsy. "Can we get something to eat?" I asked Frank.

"Sure. Want another drink?"

"Heavens, no," I said, following my mother's advice that "a woman never drinks to excess." "Nothing but ginger ale for me for the rest of the night."

To say that meat was on the buffet menu would be an understatement. Swedish meatballs, pork ribs, stroganoff on egg noodles, sliced round roast at a carving station. A mixture of braised winter vegetables topped with bacon added to the feast. Sheet cakes cut into small pieces finished the line. We loaded our plates, then huddled at a corner table and attacked the food.

Appetite satiated, I looked around at the crowd and asked Frank, "What's next?"

"Another beer," he replied. We gave up our seats and headed for the bar as a waiter swooped in and grabbed our empty plates. Halfway across the room, we were intercepted by Faye.

"Mrs. Monroe, your home is lovely," I said. "The decorations are beautiful. And dinner was delicious."

"Oh, thank you. And Henrietta, please call me Faye."

I nodded, feeling a little awestruck that she recalled my name. Up close, I remembered how young she was—probably midthirties. She was closer to my age than to her husband's.

She continued, "How are you settling in? I know you'd just moved here when we met at the rodeo. How are you handling the winter so far?"

No more blunt honesty for me. I knew better than that.

"Oh, I'm managing just fine. It is a bit windy, though, isn't it?"

Her laugh was a light bell. "Oh, yes, it's a bit windy. Just you wait. Did you manage to explore before it got too cold?"

"We hiked around the badlands looking for fossils."

Her eyes shone like luminous pools. "Oh. That's right, you're interested in that sort of thing. You're a paleontologist. Have you checked out the museum yet? In Dickerson?"

I was taken aback. "Dickerson has a museum?"

"Yes, the Dickerson History Museum. It's small, but they have dinosaur skeletons from the badlands. And other exhibits too. There's a nice collection of Indian artifacts. Some pioneer objects. Those sorts of things."

My eyes widened. "I didn't know Dickerson had a museum. I wouldn't think the town was big enough to have one." I turned to Frank. "Did you know about it?"

He shook his head. "Nope."

"It's way on the eastern side of town near some warehouses, and again, it isn't very large. But it might be right up your alley," Faye said. "I'll bet you could volunteer there if you're looking for something to do."

"Really? I'll have to check it out," I said.

"You can see people working on bones through a glass window in the back. As a matter of fact, the museum's director is here tonight. Let's see—where is he?" She scanned the room. "That's him, sitting across from the fireplace. Come on," she said with a wave of her diamonds. "I'll introduce you."

She pulled us along in her gravitational field, like planets orbiting a red giant star.

"Wally, dear, I want you to meet the Baileys," she said on approach to his chair. She patted his shoulder as he looked up at her. A guest moved away to give us some room. Moses parting the Red Sea had nothing on Faye Monroe.

"This is Frank Bailey. Frank works for George. He's a geologist. This is Wally Whitehurst."

Wally looked up at us, his cheery eyes radiating intellect. As he reached up to shake Frank's hand, I realized that crutches were leaning against his chair. Although his shoulders were broad and muscular, Wally's legs were spindly.

"And this is Frank's wife, Henrietta. She's a paleontologist. I was just telling her about the museum and thought you two should meet."

Wally turned his attention to me, his eyebrows raised. "Well, what a nice surprise." He reached over and gripped my hand. "A paleontologist, huh? Any interest in working in our lab? Digging out dinosaur bones?"

A flame of hope lit inside me, rivaling the fire roaring behind us in the hearth.

CHAPTER 12

Ignoring the holiday prerequisite of a tree, at our house Christmas preparations were negligible and decorations sparse. The wooden coat rack glowed with one strand of multicolored lights behind our front window. Homemade white paper snowflakes hung from the coat hooks with thread, my one attempt at crafting. It was good enough.

The weather continued to buffet us. Wind, sleet, snow, squalls. Inches of precipitation compounding into feet. Winds gusting at scores of miles per hour. Air pressure lowering. Polar air masses moving south, guided by the looping jet stream.

As Christmas Eve approached, I watched the snow fluttering against the windows and waited for Frank to come home. "Silent Night" scratched out from the radio in the kitchen. The days were so short now, he always arrived after dark. Our station wagon's headlights flickered in the driveway. Instead of pulling into the garage, Frank climbed out of the car and entered through the front door.

"I've got our present," he said, his eyes twinkling as he stamped his boots on the throw rug. "It's too big to maneuver inside the garage. You're going to have to help me bring it through this door."

"All right," I replied, exhilaration speeding up my pulse. The gift was not a surprise, and I had waited all day in anticipation. "Let me grab my coat and boots."

I followed him through the snowy veneer on our walkway. As he swung open the tailgate, the inside light illuminated a sizeable box filling the inside of the station wagon. "Why don't you get in the front seat and push it toward me," Frank instructed. "Then come around and help me carry it inside."

I did as he suggested, climbing into the front and bracing my feet against the dashboard. I pushed the box with all my arm strength. It slid toward Frank. He caught it with a loud groan and lowered the edge onto the ground.

"I'm coming!" I called, slamming the passenger door and scurrying around to help.

We lifted the box, grunting with strained muscles, and carried it into our living room. Frank went back outside to pull the car into the garage as I searched for a pair of heavy scissors. By the time he came through the kitchen door, I had sawed through half the box. He took off his coat and boots and joined me in the living room, cutting through the cardboard. We both gave a last tug-of-war pull, and the box fell open. Inside gleamed our Christmas gift to each other—a new RCA black-and-white nine-inch television set.

"Wow, it's so beautiful," I gushed. "I love the wooden console." I ran my hand over the unblemished oak like a child stroking a kitten.

Frank's grin widened. "Yeah, it might be too classy for this joint."

That evening, we curled up on the couch and watched *The Andy Williams Christmas Show*. As Andy crooned "It's the Most Wonderful Time of the Year" with his wife, Claudine Longet, I snuggled against Frank. "Don't they have great voices?" I asked. "They look like they're so in love when they sing together." I sighed.

"Babe," Frank said, "I'd do almost anything for you. But breaking into song is not one of them."

Christmas day passed with a litany of long-distance phone calls. Frank and his parents. Frank and each brother. The long-distance fees would be astronomical. I dialed my parents.

"Merry Christmas, Dad," I said when he answered the phone. "How's your day so far?"

"Merry Christmas, honey. Fine. Fine." He lowered his voice to a whisper. "We sure do miss you. Your mother doesn't know what to do with herself. There's no one to fuss over."

"Isn't Aunt Esther there?" I asked.

"She'll be over for dinner," he replied.

"I've got some news," I said. "Evidently there's a small museum in Dickerson, and Frank and I met the director at a Christmas party. He's invited me to work in their paleo lab."

Dad's enthusiasm reverberated across the line. "That's great, honey! Maybe you'll be able to do some research there."

"Maybe," I said. "I need to get my foot in the door first."

"Keep me posted on your progress," he said. "Wait a minute, your mom's coming out of the kitchen."

There was a shuffling noise in the background as my mother took over the receiver. "Henrietta, Merry Christmas, dear," my mom said.

"Merry Christmas, Mother. Are you making a special dinner?"

"Just a beef roast. And gravy. Carrots. Potatoes. Green bean casserole. Rolls. Pumpkin pie." She exhaled audibly. "It's quiet here without you and Frank. I hope you can make it home next year."

Ah, the guilt.

I replied, "Well, you know Frank doesn't get any vacation time until he's worked for a year."

"Oh, I know." Another exhalation. "We received your box of huckleberry jam," she said.

"I thought it might be interesting to try. It's sort of a specialty out here." I noted she didn't thank me. "We love our new hats and mittens. Thank you so much. I guess you've taken up knitting?"

"Yes, it keeps me busy. I'm glad you like them. Did you put up a tree, dear?" she asked.

I imagined the perfectly decorated tree at home in Virginia, all silver tinsel and bubble lights. The family heirloom ornaments placed in perfect symmetry.

"Well, sort of," I said. "I modified our coat rack with lights and snowflake decorations."

"Coat rack?"

"Yes. There aren't a lot of trees in North Dakota."

"Oh, I guess not. What are you and Frank having for dinner?" she asked.

I had recently discovered the wonders of Swanson TV dinners. I was not going to admit that to her, however.

"We're having turkey, mashed potatoes, peas, and baked apples," I said, picturing the color photo on the boxes in the kitchen.

"Good for you. I see you're finally learning to cook. The peas aren't from a can, are they? Canned peas are terrible."

"Oh, no, they're frozen," I said. "Frank raves about my cooking."

Frank rolled his eyes from the other end of the couch.

"What about dessert?" she asked.

"My neighbor, Janine, brought over some Christmas cookies," I said.

"Well, be sure to reciprocate, dear," she said.

"Yes, of course."

Not that I would subject poor Janine to my attempts at baking.

After a few more pleasantries, I ended the call without needing to list any more of my inadequacies. A typical holiday with my mother, albeit long distance.

CHAPTER 13

The yellow box radio on our kitchen table crackled and spit out the morning news.

> *"The Green Bay Packers beat the Dallas Cowboys 34 to 27 in yesterday's NFL Championship Game. Coach Vince Lombardi praised the team's running game and the dominance of quarterback Bart Starr. The team will play the Kansas City Chiefs in the NFL-AFL Championship Game in two weeks . . ."*

Our kitchen window vibrated from the wind, and fingers of frigid air pushed through the edges of the glass. I reached up and pulled the curtains closed in a futile attempt to keep out the chill. The radiators groaned like doomed soldiers amid a last battle. My long wool cardigan cocooned me as I hunched over the toaster, and thick socks shielded my feet from the chilly linoleum.

Frank stumbled through the kitchen door from the garage, bundled in his winter coat, extension cord in hand.

"Oh man, it is colder than a witch's tit out there. And I'm talking *inside* the garage. Thank God I plugged in the car last night."

He set the cord on the floor and pulled off his gloves. "Breakfast ready?"

I slid two pieces of toast onto a plate, buttered them, and handed the plate to him. "The radio said it's minus thirty degrees outside," I said with an involuntary shudder as I shoved two more slices of bread into the toaster.

"I don't doubt it," he said, taking a bite. "You sure you want to check out the museum today? You could wait for a warmer day."

"No. Today's the day. If I sit here for another minute listening to that wind, I'll lose my mind." The toast popped up. I speared one piece with a knife and spread the top with huckleberry jam. "Besides, I called Mr. Whitehurst, and he said to come in any weekday to meet the lab manager." I took a big bite of toast, the jam adding to the sweetness of the day.

Frank nodded as he chewed. "Well, I hope it works out for you. Call me at my office if you need me to pick you up before five o'clock."

The car engine chugged as it warmed, with the garage door lifted halfway to let out the fumes. Bundled to the hilt, I slipped into the passenger seat. Barely lukewarm air seeped through the vents from the struggling heater. Frank finished lifting the garage door, jumped into the car, and backed out of the garage. The assault was immediate. The wind slammed into the station wagon, causing it to shudder and shake. Windblown snow sandblasted the faux wood side paneling. Frank leaped out, slammed the garage door to the ground, and fought his way back to the car.

"Jesus, Mary, and Joseph," he moaned, pulling the car door shut and brushing snow off his coat. He shifted into gear. "Save me from this purgatory."

"Are you praying, Frank?" I asked with a small smile underneath my scarf.

"Just about," he said, shaking his head. We limped down the back roads toward the highway, our frigid tires thumping. "We'll pick up speed in a few minutes. It takes a couple of miles before the flat spots in the tires thaw out."

"Flat spots? I thought the rubber was just frozen."

"It is. But the air inside compresses in the cold and the tires get flat on the bottom after sitting all night. You said it was minus thirty outside."

"Well, I feel like I'm riding in the Flintstone mobile."

Monotonous fields of shimmery white expanded in every direction. Our view turned into a dizzying mirage as the snow whipped across the highway. I clicked on the car radio and searched for a station.

"And here is 'Yellow Bird' by North Dakota's native son Lawrence Welk and his orchestra . . ."

No Rolling Stones or Supremes here. Lawrence Welk's "champagne music" intermingled with the screeching wind all the way to Dickerson.

Frank dropped me off at the Dickerson History Museum with a quick kiss and headed to work. Wrapped in my parka, I scurried toward the front entrance, buffeted by the ice-tinged wind. My view of the one-story brick-and-stucco building was obscured as my eyes watered against the gale. Snow shrouded an outdoor *Ankylosaurus* statue guarding the entrance.

I yanked open the glass door and took in the museum's homey ambiance as the heated air enveloped me. A small oak desk rested inside the entry, with a guest book open for signing. According to a sign, the corridor in front of me was the Hall of Pioneer Life. Mannequins modeled nineteenth-century prairie clothing. I could see a cast-iron stove, canning jars, and old farm equipment. A replica of a Conestoga wagon stood at the end of the hall.

Behind me, the door opened and another winter-garbed person blew inside. She unwrapped the scarf around her face and grinned.

"Good morning! Welcome to the museum," she said.

The new blast of air caused me to shiver. "Thank you. I'm here to meet the lab manager. Mr. Whitehurst told me to stop by."

"That would be Hans Olson. I'll take you to his office," she said, the crow's-feet around her eyes crinkling. She removed her hat and shook out her curly gray hair. "This way."

We passed through the pioneer hall and entered a hall with prairie animals. A taxidermist had been busy. The stuffed menagerie included a pronghorn, several prairie dogs set in different poses, a prairie chicken in a territorial display, and even a coyote.

"I'm Mary Tremaine," the woman said. "I work here as a volunteer."

"Nice to meet you. I'm Henrietta Ballantine. I'm hoping to volunteer here too. In the paleo lab."

She nodded. "Wonderful! That's where I work. It'll be nice to have some company. I help with school tours too. I can show you the ropes after you meet with Hans."

We squeezed down a narrow hall, past a door stenciled with DIRECTOR. "That's Mr. Whitehurst's office," she said. She pointed ahead to a door marked PRIVATE. "And that's Hans's office." Mary knocked.

"Yeah?" called a male voice.

"Hans? It's Mary. Someone's here to see you."

The door opened and Mary melted away behind me.

My first impression of Hans was that he was a hippie version of Ichabod Crane. Tall, lanky, a middle-aged scarecrow, he was way too old to be sporting a long ponytail, in my opinion.

"Who are you?" he asked, not inviting me inside. The space behind him resembled a cross between an office and a utility closet.

"Hello. I'm Dr. Henrietta Ballantine. Mr. Whitehurst told me to come meet you."

He folded his arms across his flannel shirt. Frown lines darkened his brow. "Oh, yeah. The *woman* paleontologist, right?"

I stared right back at him. "Yes, I'm actually a paleobotanist. I was hoping to volunteer in the paleo lab."

"Do you have lab experience?"

"Yes, I worked in a lab at the Smithsonian."

He smirked. "Well, la-di-da. Have you worked on vertebrates?"

"I have, but not on dinosaurs. I spent several summers working on fish fossils."

He stared at me unabashedly. The stuffy air began to press in on me, and I started to sweat inside my coat.

"Can you lift heavy boxes of bones?"

"Sure."

I wondered if he had asked Mary that question.

"It's not just working on bones, ya know. The volunteers might be asked to clean the halls. Or empty the trash."

"I can do that."

He took another moment, studying me like a lab rat.

"You can start on a trial basis. We're not the Smithsonian, but we do have *standards* in our lab. Plus, you'll have to help with the children when teachers bring their classes."

I think I'd rather empty the trash, I did not say.

"Wonderful. Thank you," I replied.

Wunnerful, wunnerful. That Lawrence Welk music must be getting to me.

———

The Paleontology Preparation Laboratory was glass-fronted, its wide windows enabling visitors to watch as technicians worked to extract bones from the encasing rock. Mary was alone in the lab, bent over a specimen under a large magnifier. She noticed my approach and sent me a big smile. Standing up, she motioned for me to come through a side door.

"Heigh-ho, I guess you passed Hans's appraisal?"

"Yes, I'm cleared to work here on a 'trial basis,'" I said.

"Oh, he tells everyone that." She pulled open the double doors of a tall wooden cabinet along the back wall. "You can put your coat in here. And your purse too. This will keep the dust off everything. Just grab any lab coat in there."

I hung my coat, scarf, and purse on a hook and pulled out a white lab coat. I slipped it on over my clothes, buttoning the front.

"Did you bring your lunch? You can put it in the icebox," Mary said, motioning to a full-size Hotpoint refrigerator.

"I brought a sandwich in my purse." I reached into the cabinet, grabbed my purse, and pulled out my sandwich. I crossed to the refrigerator and opened the door. "Wow, the fridge is almost empty," I said.

"It gets more use in the summer." She continued, "The restrooms are right out the door you came in and down that short hallway. The side door to the museum is at the end, but you need a key to enter there. All the visitors come through the front."

Next to the refrigerator, beakers dried in a rack hanging over a utility sink. Several wooden crates occupied the far corner. Mary motioned to one of the crates.

"Here are some of the specimens we're working on. Bones of a *Triceratops*. Just grab a chunk that looks interesting to you."

"All right," I said, squatting down to examine my choices. I picked up what I thought might be part of a rib.

"Ooh, that's a good one. Now, just pull up a chair and join me. The tools are in these drawers under the workbenches."

Along the front windows, a row of tables lined the wall. Mary turned and opened one of the long drawers underneath her station. Brushes, picks, probes, scraping knives, and hand lenses rolled around inside.

I grabbed a chair, rolled it along the floor, and settled in next to her.

"Do other people work in the lab?" I asked.

"Yes, but not so many in the winter. Right now, there are a few high school students who come in after school a few days a week. But in the summer, there are a lot more people. Teachers and college students on their summer breaks. The museum runs camps for children during the summer too, so it's more crowded then. That's how I started here. My husband and I were teachers, and we'd come over from Minnesota to work during the summers. When we retired, we moved here."

I set my fossil in front of me and swiveled a large arm-mounted magnifying glass above it. I eyeballed it through the magnifier and tested the surrounding rock with a steel pick. The matrix was quite hard.

"Looks like I can use an air scribe. Do we have those?"

Mary pointed. "Right in the drawer there."

I slid open a drawer and, finding a pencil-like electric air scribe, plugged it in and switched it on. The tiny probe vibrated with a whine. I pressed it onto the specimen, removing rock from bone, one minuscule chip at a time.

"You retired and could have moved anywhere? And you moved to North Dakota?" I asked Mary. "On purpose?"

From the corner of my eye, I saw her give me an enigmatic look.

"It'll grow on ya. Just wait and see."

CHAPTER 14

It was one of those rare crystalline mornings when the wind miraculously ceased. The sun peered above the eastern horizon, casting a golden tinge over the snow-covered landscape. Iridescent sun dogs flanked the sun like glowing crescent rainbows, evidence of ice crystals in the atmosphere. In North Dakota–speak, today was another day when "the temperature outside was below." As in below zero. From the passenger seat, I pulled my hat down over my ears, tucking in my long braid, and watched my breath condense into clouds inside our car.

Frank's fingers tapped on the steering wheel, and as he drove, he muttered to himself.

I turned toward him. "Are you ready for your presentation?" I asked.

"Yeah, I think so. I've got my map and cross-sections ready to show George."

I reached forward and swiveled the vent to blast the tepid air toward my face. "Can't you tell me a little bit about your new prospect?"

He glanced over at me, huffing out a cloud of impatience. "It's all confidential. You know that. I can tell you that it's in Montana."

"Tell me something general about the geology. Without telling me the exact location."

"Well, it's a whole new idea for a play," he said, the edges of his lips lifting. "Nothing like it has been drilled in the Williston Basin before, at least as far as I've seen. The well would be a true wildcat."

"A wildcat?"

"An exploratory well. One that's not in an established field."

"Oh. What's so different about it?"

"It's a unique type of stratigraphic trap. I've seen something like it in the Appalachians. I'm proposing an analog that hasn't been recognized here yet."

"Sounds promising."

"Yeah, it has high potential. At least I think so. And here's the amazing part—if Monroe Petroleum decides to drill it, and we hit oil, I'll earn an overriding royalty interest. The percentage isn't high, but even so, I could stand to make a lot of money if the well comes in."

"Well, I'm all for that!" I said, grinning at him. "Maybe we'll be celebrating tonight?"

"Oh, not yet. This is only the first step. Fortunately, Monroe Petroleum already owns the land leases in the area. But first, I've got to convince George."

"I'm sure you will, honey. You can be very persuasive." I reached over and gave him a side hug. "After all, you convinced me to marry you."

We reached the museum's parking lot, tires rolling over the packed snow, just as Hans climbed out of his truck. Frank pulled our car to the end of the sidewalk, and I leaned over and gave him a big smooch just as Hans walked by. Seeing us, he made an obvious gagging pantomime as he passed.

Frank smiled. "How's ole Hans going to irritate you this week?"

"Oh my God, who knows? He lives to torment me, I think."

Frank chuckled. "Yeah, well, you used to say the same thing about me. Don't go falling for him now."

"Oh, pah-leese," I said, swatting him on the shoulder. "Don't make me nauseous this early in the morning."

"I'll see you at five."

"Seriously, good luck today, honey," I said, cracking open my car door. "I know your presentation will be terrific."

I skirted across the icy sidewalk, my breath fogging my glasses, and scurried inside the museum. My fingers were numb inside my mittens. Bypassing the pioneer life and prairie ecology exhibits, I passed through the Indian artifacts section, which led to the dinosaurs. Faye Monroe's collection was far superior to the museum's. A bison hide served as a draped backdrop to the exhibit, with arrowheads and hand axes placed on its fur. Mandan and Hidatsa pottery, bulbous in shape, with curved rims and decorated with flutes and grooves, comprised most of the exhibit. Several old photographs of Indians wrapped in blankets completed the display, the indigenous people staring despondently at the camera lens. I moved on, chastened by the donor labels, not a native name among them.

As I entered the now-familiar Hall of Paleontology, my spirits lifted. For a small museum, the dinosaur collection was quite varied. The skeletons of *Stegosaurus*, *Triceratops*, and *Edmontosaurus* perched on pedestals as if in suspended animation. Cases displayed dinosaur eggs, dinosaur claws, dinosaur teeth, and dinosaur horns. A duck-bill, coprolite hills, and a ceratopsid frill. Dinosaur footprints marched sideways across one wall. I considered myself lucky to look over this bounty from my spot in the prep lab.

"Morning, Henrietta." Mary looked up from her specimen as I came through the side door. "Good to see you. I missed you the past few days."

"Hi, Mary. Yeah, Frank was at a rig," I said, "and even though he rode with someone else, I couldn't get the car out of the garage. There was too much snow piled up in front of the door. And honestly, I was tired of shoveling." I pulled open the door to the coat cabinet and began to remove my outerwear.

"Well, that's North Dakota," she said. "Shovel and swat."

I laughed, remembering summertime's voracious mosquitoes. "Isn't that the truth."

She continued, "Wally was out too. It was pretty quiet around here."

"Oh? Was he sick?"

"I don't know, but I'm worried about him," she said, setting down her pick. "You know he had polio when he was a child. That makes any illness more complicated. And he's such a sweetheart. I'd hate to hear he's ailing."

I closed the cabinet door with a click. "If he's not back today, why don't you call him? I mean, as a friend and coworker who's worried about him?"

A blush crept up Mary's face. "Oh, I don't think I could do that."

I squinted my eyes at her. "Why not?" I asked. "It's 1967. A woman can call a man to check on him."

She shook her head. "I'm not that forward. Let's ask Hans. Maybe he's heard something."

"Well, I don't think it would hurt for you to seize the day. *Carpe diem*, you know? Especially if you think he's a 'sweetheart.'"

Her cheeks flushed pink.

I spied a new wooden crate in the corner. "What are we working on today? Something new?"

She brushed back a strand of frizz and nodded. "Dinosaur skin impressions, supposedly. Inside those blocks." She pointed toward the crate. "We have to scrape the sediment away very carefully so we don't scratch them."

"Wow, cool!" I said, walking over to the box. I leaned over and weighed my choices. Hunks of tan sandstone moldered in the crate. I selected a fist-size piece and took it to my worktable. Swiveling the magnifier, I set the rock beneath it and reached into the drawer for my brush and dental pick.

"I'm sure Hans will come through soon and give us instructions," Mary said in a low voice.

"Oh yes, I'm sure that Horrible Hans won't miss his chance to lord something over us," I answered in a dramatic whisper.

Mary stifled a laugh. "You are terrible, Henrietta."

"No. He is."

The friable sandstone slowly yielded to the pressure of my pick, layer by delicate layer. like peeling an atomic onion. Powder floated in the air as we worked alongside each other. The scritch of our picks mixed with the low droning of the farm report emanating from the radio behind us.

As if he'd been waiting for an off-stage cue, Hans snaked his way through the lab door.

"Good morning, girls. My God, what a mess," he said, stepping over to us. "Why not swipe the piles of discards into the trash bin as you work? We do have cleanliness standards, you know."

"Thank you, Hans. I've never worked in a lab before," I said, putting saccharine in my voice. My eyes remained fixed on my specimen under the magnifier.

"Oh, I know you've worked at the Smithsonian, Henrietta. God knows everyone's been told," he said. From the corner of my eye, I saw him stare down his nose and flick his ponytail off his shoulder.

Mary cleared her throat. "Have you heard any news about Mr. Whitehurst?"

His attention turned to her. "What? Oh. No. He doesn't report to me." He sniffed. "Now, how are the skin impression blocks coming along?"

"I don't see anything in mine yet," Mary said.

"I've just started on mine. I wasn't here at the end of last week," I said.

"Ah, yes, you had a nice long snow-stay, didn't you?"

"Well, we had that blizzard. Frank was gone, and I couldn't shovel all the snow."

His face turned incredulous. "Blizzard? You call that a blizzard? You should have been here last March. Now *that* was a blizzard. The blizzard of the century. That would've blown your mind." He turned his attention back to the blocks on the table. "Be careful with these. It's slow going if you do them correctly."

"Where are the skin impressions from?" I asked, trying to modulate my voice. "What age are they?"

"Why don't you leave that to the dinosaur paleontologists," Hans replied, baring his teeth at me in what might have been a grin. "If we find any fossil shrubbery, I'll be sure to let you know."

"Gee, thanks," I said flatly.

"Anyway, there's a group of kids coming in this morning for a tour. I was wondering if you girls could help out."

"I'd be happy to," Mary said. "I saw it on the calendar. They're third graders—my specialty."

"Perfect. They should be here soon." He turned on his heel and left us, the door slamming closed with a thud.

"I guess he needed to crawl back under his rock," I said. "Have you ever noticed that his bicuspids are very pointy? Like a mangy dog?"

Mary looked at me over her reading glasses. "He *is* the lab manager, you know. We *do* work for him."

"We're volunteers, Mary. What's he going to do? Fire us?"

She replied, "I know we're not paid, but after Paul died, this work saved me. It gave me a purpose. I wouldn't want to be told that my services are no longer needed."

I reached over and squeezed her hand. "I'm sorry. I do know what you mean. I'll tone it down. This place has saved my sanity too. But if Hans calls us 'girls' one more time, I'm going to beat him over the head with my rock hammer."

Muffled voices distracted us from the other side of our glass enclosure. A throng of children raced into the gallery. Hans was with them, arms waving in an attempt to corral them.

"Calm down, please. Inside voices," called out a frazzled-looking woman who I assumed was their teacher.

"Oh, the children are here," Mary said, rising from her seat. A smile spread across her face.

A chorus of giggles bounced off the walls as the tots skipped down the walkway toward us. Sticky fingers pressed up against our glass window, leaving smudgy prints. Wide eyes ogled us. Mary waved to the children. My skin prickled. I felt just like a caged beast in a zoo.

At day's end, Mary and I shrugged on our coats and crushed our heads inside woolen hats. I closed the door to the coat closet with a click.

"Do you ever get tired of putting all this stuff on?" I asked, winding my scarf around my neck.

"Oh, I've been doing it my whole life. You'll get used to it after a few winters here," she said.

Mary flicked the wall switch, extinguishing the lab lights. We exited the side door and walked through the dinosaur hall.

"I hope Frank's meeting went well today," I said as I passed the *Stegosaurus.*

"Tell him good luck from me," Mary said. We rounded past the pioneer relics. With a wave, she slipped out the front door toward her car.

I waited inside the vestibule for Frank. Slices of cold air oozed like icy ribbons around the door edges, and condensation dripped down the inside of the glass. Our station wagon swooped in with a fishtail of slush and gravel. As I opened the door, the usual blast of frigid air hit my face. My breath exhaled as a cloud. On approach, I could see Frank's jaw set in a hard line through the windshield. I hurried over and climbed into the passenger seat.

Frank turned toward me with a deep frown, his gloved fingers gripping the steering wheel.

Not a good sign.

"How was your day? How did your meeting go?" I asked.

He spun the wheel and pulled out onto the road. "He's farming it out."

"What?"

"George. He's farming out my prospect."

"What does that mean?" I asked.

Frank's eyes bore ahead. He ran his left hand over his face. "The meeting today? He'd arranged for Warhawk Development to be there. Without telling me. Monroe Petroleum won't be drilling my prospect. George made a deal with Warhawk, and they'll be the ones drilling the well. We'll retain a small royalty if the well discovers oil."

"Is that bad news? At least your well will be drilled. That's got to be a positive thing, right?"

He squinted into the lowering sun. "Yes, the well will be drilled. Warhawk will put up most of the money. And if it's successful, they'll earn most of the profit. Monroe will earn a small share. And any thoughts of me getting an overriding royalty interest have flown out the window."

"We'll be all right. We don't need the money, do we?"

"Henrietta, you don't understand. An overriding interest could have brought us a lot of money. I'm talking *a lot* if the prospect hits big. It could have paid out for years, as long as the well produced oil."

"But your idea will get tested. That's what's important here, right? If it pans out, you'll be able to use your concept for other prospects, yes?"

"I'm not sure I'll even get to see the data. Warhawk's geologists will take over the well. And even if I'm allowed to go on a logging run, I'll just be an observer. I'll have no say in how the well gets drilled."

"I'm sorry, honey." I slid next to him on the seat and rested my head on his shoulder.

"The thing that really burns my ass is that after the meeting, I heard George laughing on the phone, saying the prospect is a 'pie in the sky deal' and how lucky we are to farm it out. It goes to show you how much an engineer knows about exploration."

"And yet, he's running the place," I said.

"Yep, he's the boss. Unfortunately."

CHAPTER 15

February's icy grip made the previous months' weather feel like practice for the real thing. The wind was such a constant presence I thought my eardrums would never stop vibrating. A massive snowdrift piled up against the windward side of our house like an alpine glacier. If we wanted to, we could have climbed up its frozen surface onto our roof. In contrast, the roof itself was devoid of snow, removed by the gusts to form horizontally driven pellets. In Dickerson, a field next to the elementary school had been purposefully flooded. The water froze on contact, forming a rink on which the children ice-skated during recess. How they managed to balance vertically on skates without being blown over was beyond me.

Frank continued with his one-man Laurel and Hardy routine of getting our car ready each morning. It took inordinate amounts of time in the subfreezing cold. Plugging in the car, struggling with the garage door while being buffeted by the wind, unplugging the car, warming up the car, pulling it out of the garage, then racing to shut the garage door. I felt sorry for him but offered no help—it was just too blessed cold. Bundled to the hilt, my sweaters and coat giving me the breadth of the Pillsbury Doughboy, I raced out at the last minute to pop in the front seat.

Inside the museum, the halls struggled to warm, and the glass window enclosing the paleo lab was cold to the touch. Mary and I plugged a space heater into an extension cord and huddled in front of its metal vent. Some days I wore work gloves just to keep my hands warm.

One morning I arrived to find Mary and Wally Whitehurst hunched over a specimen, deep in conversation. The casual manner in which he leaned toward her, his hand on the back of her chair, gave me pause. When they heard me come through the door, they pulled apart from each other, and he removed his hand.

"Good morning," I said. "You're both here bright and early."

Wally cleared his throat. "I was just looking at this fossil turtle that Mary is working on."

My coat found its usual hook in the cabinet. "Yeah, it's a nice specimen. And prepared expertly, I might add," I said, smiling toward Mary.

Wally rose to his feet and grabbed his crutches. "I'll let you two get to work. Henrietta, sometime this morning, can you come to my office?"

"Of course," I said. "I'll be there in a few minutes."

"Take your time. No rush," he said. He strode out the door, his crutches clicking on the linoleum. Mary and I watched his back as he crossed the dinosaur hall.

"So . . . it looks like you called and checked on Wally after all?" I asked.

She gave me a sheepish grin. "Yes. I did. I thought about what you said and decided to 'carpe diem' as you put it. He'd been down with a cold. One thing led to another, and I invited him to my place for a home-cooked meal."

My eyes widened. "And you never told me? You sly fox, you!"

She had the decency to look embarrassed. "Well, there's not that much to tell."

"Oh, please. You two looked pretty chummy when I came in. Is it safe to say the two of you are an item?"

"I guess you might say that. But it's early days yet," she said with a shy grin.

"Well, good for you!" I said. "If it gets serious, I'm going to want details. But right now, I guess I'll see what Wally wants to talk to me about. Do you have any idea?"

"I'll let him tell you," she said.

"I'm not in trouble, am I?"

She laughed and dismissed me with a wave of her hand. "No, of course not."

I left the lab and crossed back through the dinosaur hall, feeling the skulls' hollow-eyed stares at my back, as if they too were wondering why Mr. Whitehurst wanted to see me.

The museum's front door rattled as I cut across the entrance hall. Through the glass, I saw new snow blowing across the sidewalk, erasing my incoming footprints from minutes ago. The sky seemed to sigh under an opaque shroud of gray stratus. I shivered and continued past the covered wagon, the prairie dogs, and the coyote. Down the short hallway, I knocked on the director's door.

"Come in!"

Mr. Whitehurst sat behind his metal desk. Filing cabinets stretched along the far wall. Large framed color photographs displaying a variety of Great Plains creatures—a bison, prairie dogs, a pronghorn antelope—decorated his walls.

"Henrietta, have a seat."

I scooched into a chair in front of the desk. "Wow, these photographs are amazing," I said, rubbernecking around the room. "In color too!"

He beamed. "Thank you. I took them."

I pulled back in surprise. "You did?"

"Yes, sure did."

"Is that a ferret?" I pointed, remembering a sketch in my wildlife book.

"Yes, a black-footed ferret. I was lucky with that one—it's pretty rare. They eat prairie dogs, and I happened to see him when I was photographing that colony over there." He indicated another frame. "When I was younger I didn't let these legs slow me down. I'd drive out of town and make do with my crutches. Not so easy these days, though."

"Mary told me that you had polio as a child," I said, then bit my lip. *Was that rude?*

He nodded. "I did. Caught it when I was nine years old. Spent months away from my family. They quarantined us back then. It's one reason I left New York. Lots of bad memories."

"I'm sorry to hear that. You became a scientist, though, right?"

"I wanted to study geology but knew I couldn't do the fieldwork. Instead, I went into chemistry. I came out here for a teaching job and, well, it's the old story. Met a girl, decided to stay."

I smiled. "I knew from your accent that you weren't from around here."

"When I first came out here, I could hardly understand anyone. All those 'ooh yeahs and 'you betchas.' And I have to say, they had trouble understanding my Bronx accent too," he said.

"But you were able to teach high school?"

"Yes, until it became too difficult for me to physically stand up for long periods. So I had to retire from that, but I took this job, which kept me going after my wife passed." He cleared his throat. "Anyway, I didn't ask you to come to hear all of that. I wanted to ask you about summer fieldwork. I know it's early, but I'm starting to think about the summer field crew. I thought you might be interested."

My heart awakened in my chest. "I might be! What would it entail?"

"We send a small crew, usually about four or five people. We can't afford more than that. With two pickup trucks full of supplies. The team is headed by Dr. Theo Small. He's a vertebrate paleontologist from Dakota State. He usually brings a grad student or two with him. And of course, Hans is part of the team."

Ugh.

"I know you have digging experience . . ." he said.

"I do, yes. What's the timing?"

"Hard to say exactly. It depends on the weather. June through August, of course. Maybe earlier. There's no water out there, so the crew hauls five days' worth with them. They drive out on Mondays and come back on Fridays. Everything is restocked over the weekend, then they go out again. It's rustic camping—tents, latrine, no showers."

"That sounds good to me. And we'd be digging for dinosaurs?"

"Yes. Last summer the crew discovered a site, and they'll be continuing there this year. It's a bone graveyard, from what I hear. Pieces of several different species in one spot. The crew extracted some bones last year and brought them to the storage barn, but most of those are still in their jackets."

"So we'd be using the same campsite as last year?"

"Exactly. Which is nice because you won't have to spend time prospecting for a new site. You can get right to work."

"And I'd be field labor?" I asked, my eyebrows rising.

He pursed his lips. "Well . . . what I had in mind . . . that is . . . yes, you'd be working on the dig too . . . but what I thought is . . . they'll need a cook."

I took a moment.

"A cook?"

"Yes. You'd be paid, of course. You *can* cook, can't you?"

"Well, I'm not exactly known for my cooking skills."

"It's not like you'd be making gourmet meals. Lots of peanut butter sandwiches. It would mostly be opening cans and warming up food on a camp stove. And doing the dishes."

"The dishes?"

"Just the pans and utensils. Everyone will scrub out their own mess kit. With so little water, you'd be scrubbing with wet sand and doing minimal rinsing. On the weekends, you'd need to give the pots a good wash. There's also meal planning and making the shopping list."

"Would I be doing the grocery shopping too?"

"Yes. With a budget. You'd be going to the store on Saturdays anyway, wouldn't you? To shop for your husband?"

"I suppose," I said. I took a deep breath and let the silence settle for a minute. "Who cooked last year?"

"They took turns. Which I gather was not ideal. I think it would be better to have one person in charge."

I would be in charge. Of cooking, cleaning, and shopping. Wow, what a proposition. My PhD would finally be put to good use.

Mr. Whitehurst offered a satisfactory look and leaned back in his chair. "Just think about it. And I assume you'll want to ask your husband's permission first."

Ah yes. Mrs. Frank Bailey, cook, dishwasher, and grocery shopper. I may as well be listed in the Betty Crocker cookbook after all.

CHAPTER 16

The letter from my dad brought memories of past explorations as well as a gentle reminder that I needed to push forward with new research. He wrote like he spoke, with one long breath. A wave of homesickness fell over me as I read.

March 20, 1967

Dear Henrietta,

Happy Spring Equinox. Exciting news! I'm enclosing the first draft of a publication to be submitted to the Vertebrate Paleontology Bulletin—I'm one of the co-authors. The fish fossil that you brought back from Olduvai Gorge—the unique one that looked like a cartilaginous impression with the bulbous head—we've finally finished collaborating with Larry Waller—he's an up-and-coming young vertebrate paleontologist here at the museum—studied under Ostrom—you'd like him—and we've named it a new species. It is indeed a variety of lungfish, Class Dipnoi. The genus is Protopterus, new species africanus. You can read the details. Note your name listed in the acknowledgments section.

I'm interested to hear about your research. What are you working on at your museum? I'm sure you're making great strides with the Cretaceous fauna and flora.

Your mother is knitting up a storm. The church has a ministry to donate scarves to the needy. It keeps her off the streets, so to speak. The daffodils are peeking out in the yard, so by the time she's finished, no one will need them. I don't tell her this, of course.

My regards to Frank.

Love,
Dad

A wave of guilt pulsed through me. I had exaggerated the scope of my work in letters to my dad. I didn't want to let him down when he was so keen to see me succeed. I knew that preparing bones without knowing their history or provenance did not qualify as research. So I hadn't bothered to enlighten him about that part.

Eight months had passed since I had seen my parents. Phone calls and letters aside, I missed my dad's single-minded ramblings. I even missed my mother's manic perfectionism. And of course, my Aunt Esther's gentle presence.

The middle of March in Virginia brought the first whispers of spring—crocuses and hyacinths poking green shoots up from the ground, dogwoods and azaleas beginning to bud. Not so in North Dakota. Today was Saturday, and the air temperature hovered just below the freezing mark. Yet the sun beamed down like a blessing, unimpeded by any clouds. Frank and I walked along our plowed road, encased in our requisite five layers of outerwear. Drifts of snow remained piled against the neighborhood houses, refusing to melt. Several weeks had passed since Mr. Whitehurst made his offer, and I had not mentioned it to Frank. Instead, mulling it over in my mind, I weighed the opportunity to dig versus the audacity of him wanting me to play housekeeper.

"Where should we go for lunch?" Frank asked, giving me his lopsided grin.

"Where o' where? So many choices," I replied from under my scarf. Clara's Bar and Grill was as busy as it would ever be. A colorful array of pickup trucks parked diagonally in front of the rectangular building lined up like finger bones. We stepped inside to the clanking and murmuring of the lunch crowd. The scent of frying grease clung to the air. Shelves located to our right served as a mini-market, stacked with canned goods and rudimentary drugstore supplies. A refrigerator offered milk and cold sodas—Coca-Cola, Fresca, Tab, or Hires root beer. The restaurant was located to the left. Four booths with cracked vinyl seats and six metal tables filled the dining area. A wooden bar stretched across the far back wall. Polka music blared from speakers in the corners.

Did they ever play anything else?

All but two of the tables were taken.

"Grab yourselves a table. I'll be right with you." The aforementioned Clara, who doubled as owner, waitress, hostess, and bartender, waved us in. She was dressed in her customary white apron, jeans, and flannel shirt.

"More choices," Frank whispered. He waved at a couple of roustabouts eating lunch at a booth as we walked past. We sat at one of the empty tables, grabbed a menu for no reason, and turned our coffee cups right side up.

After a few minutes, Clara walked over, carrying a coffeepot. "Do you want coffee or a pop?"

"Coffee, please," we chorused.

"Today's special is pork chops and sauerkraut. It comes with carrots. You want two?"

"Yes, ma'am," Frank said as I nodded in agreement.

"Good." She stomped away and tossed an order slip through a window opening to the unseen kitchen in the back.

"No choices there," I whispered to Frank.

Frank took a sip of coffee and grimaced.

"That good, huh?"

"Remember the coffee we drank in Africa? If that was a ten, then this is a negative two. At best."

"Oh, I remember the coffee in Africa quite well," I said, lifting my cup. Frank had followed me to Olduvai Gorge five years ago. "It would be insane to even try to compare to that." I took a bitter swallow as two full plates were plunked in front of us. Hot gravy smothered the pork chop, giving off a fragrant steam.

"Here you go. Two specials. Anything else?" Clara barked.

"No, thanks."

"Taste your carrots before you salt 'em," she advised before she bustled away.

Frank looked down. "I guess it would be too much for her to ask if I wanted gravy. I hate gravy."

"Try to scrape it off."

"How do you scrape off gravy? It gets in the pores."

I sighed. "Jeez, I don't know. Do you want me to ask her to take it back?"

"Hell no. I want to live," Frank said, poking at the gravy with his knife.

"Don't be grumpy," I said, cutting my pork chop into pieces. "We're celebrating!"

He nodded. "I guess so. My well's going to spud next week."

I looked up at him and squinted my eyes. "Spud? Like a potato?"

"Oh, sorry—begin drilling."

"How long will it take to drill?" I asked, taking a bite of pork chop. I thought the gravy was delicious, which I did not mention.

"A few months, at least. Probably into midsummer. Warhawk's geologist is actually a pretty decent guy, so I'll be included in all the logging runs."

"That's good news! You'll be able to see the data."

Frank speared a forkful of sauerkraut. "Yeah, a minor victory for me, since if the well comes in, Monroe will get a small royalty. And I'll personally get squat."

"If the well finds oil, you'll get the satisfaction of knowing your prospect was a good one. And I'll sing your praises, even if no one else does."

Frank grinned. "I've heard your singing. You don't need to bother."

"Gee, thanks," I said. My mind had been working feverishly on how to present my summer offer to Frank. I inhaled and leaned across the table. "Speaking of summer . . . Mr. Whitehurst offered me a summer job. As part of a field crew digging for dinosaurs. He also wants to hire me as the cook."

Frank choked on his bite of sauerkraut. He reached for his coffee cup, took a big swallow, and cleared his throat. "He wants *you* to be the cook? Did he ask you if you *could* cook?"

"Well, not exactly. Anyway, it would be five days out in the badlands and home on weekends to resupply. The site is fairly remote, evidently. We'd be hauling our food and water. You know, rustic camping. The usual."

Frank studied me, his eyes wary.

"I was wondering if you'd mind if I went?" I continued.

"How many weeks is it?"

I chewed on a carrot. "Not sure. Depends on the weather. The field season is so short here. I mean, you'll be out in the field too for your logging runs."

"Yeah, but not for the whole summer."

"I can make dinners for you and freeze them. With my amazing cooking abilities," I said with a grin, trying to lighten the mood.

He wiped his lips with a napkin. His forehead creased. "I was hoping we could spend some more time hiking together. Exploring the badlands on the weekends."

"We could still hike on Sundays," I said to his darkening face.

"What about Saturdays?" he asked.

"I'd have to go grocery shopping for the crew on Saturdays. For the next week."

"Good God. After all that, you'd probably just want to collapse on Sundays. So there goes the entire summer," he said with a frown.

I knew when I started the conversation that Frank would balk at my leaving. Why was it always the woman's job to accommodate, to make concessions?

I sat back and folded my arms. "I knew you wouldn't be happy, but listen, this is an opportunity I don't want to pass up. I can only scrape at bones in a lab for so long before being bored out of my gourd."

Frank rubbed his forehead and squinted. "So you're bored here? In North Dakota?"

"A little bit, yeah. You have to admit, it's been a long winter."

He picked up his fork and stabbed a carrot. "Seems you've already made up your mind. When would you start?"

"First week of June, if the weather holds."

He took his time replying, assessing me through his piercing eyes. "Anything I can do to help you get ready?"

"Oh, yes," I said, giving him a sly wink. "I'm sure I can think of something we'll need to do a lot before I leave."

We were still newlyweds, after all.

Frank reached for my hand on our trek back home and gave it a squeeze, which helped reassure my anxious heart. We swung our clasped hands back and forth as we passed the town playground, the snow underfoot trampled and sooty. A toddler, bundled in a snowsuit, attempted to slide sideways down the metal slide. Laughing and screeching, he tumbled like a jelly roll into his mother's open arms. We waved to her as we walked by, and she sent us a gloved wave back.

The little boy held Frank's attention. "Do you think you'd be more comfortable talking about having kids if we lived closer to our families?"

Where had that suggestion come from?

The sun's rays refracted off the snow, sending a glare into my face. I squinted into the sunlight. "Oh, Frank, I don't know. Why?"

"We don't have to stay in North Dakota for the long haul, you know. There's a new trend opening up called the Tuscaloosa Trend. The major oil companies have had some big discoveries in it. When it takes off, they're going to need to hire more experienced geologists. From what I've heard, there's potential for big payouts."

"Where's the trend?"

"Louisiana."

I stopped and looked up at him. "Louisiana? From the frigid north to the sultry south, huh?"

Frank shrugged. "It's just a possibility. We'd be a little closer to our families, at least by plane. And maybe you could get a job there. Or, you know, be more comfortable talking about kids."

My stomach began to churn, but not from the pork chop.

CHAPTER 17

Winter slowly released its grip, like a beast with embedded claws awakening from hibernation. Temperatures rose, and a few glorious middays in early April finally cracked the freezing mark. Inside the paleo lab the outside world receded. Mary and I agreed to silence the radio, as we found both the polka music and the weather report repetitious. My mind settled into the background murmur of the air scribe as loose rock slivers surrounding a *Triceratops* horn blasted past my fingertips.

I switched off the scribe and picked up one of my brushes. Mary hunched over a hunk of sandstone, her neck a fishhook. Gripping a dental pick in her skilled hand, she flung away sand grains. With a frown on her face, she emitted a small sigh.

"Maybe it's time you gave up on that block," I said. "I tossed mine back in the bin long ago. What makes Hans think there are dinosaur skin imprints inside anyway? I think it's just something he made up to annoy us."

She looked up. "It's certainly wearing my patience. Maybe I'll go back to the turtle carapace. I was making better headway with that."

I nodded at her as I flicked my brush, separating tiny rock particles from the horn. "Good idea. I wonder if the leg bones are inside the turtle shell?"

She stared off into space, her eyes unfocused, as if her mind were elsewhere.

"Maybe there's a skull too," I said, studying her.

"Uh-huh," she said, continuing to stare into the dinosaur hall, void of visitors at this hour.

"Maybe the turtle had wings," I persisted, trying to get a reaction from her. She continued to ignore me. "Are you all right?" I finally asked. "You seem distracted."

She snapped back and looked at me. "What? Oh, I'm fine. I'm just, you know, worried about Wally. He doesn't seem himself lately."

"How so?"

"He's being somewhat cagey with me. He's planning some trips but won't say what they're for. I heard him speaking on the phone to someone. But when I asked him about it, he just clammed up."

"Could he be visiting his kids? He has grown children, doesn't he?"

"Yes," she said, sweeping a lock of gray hair away from her eyes. "A son in Denver and a daughter in Minneapolis. But I think if he were planning to visit them, he'd just tell me."

"Maybe he's fundraising for the museum. Does he ever travel for that?"

The lines between her eyes accentuated. "Yes, sometimes. I guess I could ask him. But again, why not just tell me?"

"It seems to me that you and Wally have moved from casual friends to a committed couple?" I asked, raising my eyebrows.

Mary blushed crimson. "You could say that he's stolen my heart."

"That thief!" I teased as a lump formed in my throat. "Seriously, that's so sweet. Wally seems like a stand-up kind of guy. I can't imagine he has another girlfriend stashed somewhere."

She shook her head. "I'm worried that it's something medical and he doesn't want to upset me. It seems we've finally found each other, and now I don't know what's going to happen next."

I reached over, grabbed her hand, and squeezed it. "I'm sorry, Mary," I said. "But none of us can know what's going to happen next."

If I only knew.

The *Triceratops* horn was a magnificent specimen, but preparing it was slow going. A giant Cracker Jack prize waiting to be revealed for geological periods. Two weeks later I was still working on its extraction. I stared through the huge magnifying lens as I slid my fingertip over the fossil to distinguish the edge of the horn from the grittiness of the encasing sandstone. Rock flakes skittered in the air as I carefully chipped them away. Hearing the side door open, I quieted my electric drill and looked up.

"Ah, Henrietta, there you are!" Mr. Whitehurst shoved the door open with his shoulder and pulled himself into the room.

"Mr. Whitehurst, so good to see you. Mary mentioned you've been traveling?"

"Ah, yes, I had some business to attend to in Minneapolis."

Mary followed behind him, removing her coat and hat. Mr. Whitehurst walked over and settled himself in a chair next to me, resting his crutches between his knobby knees.

He continued. "I knew you'd done some fieldwork, but Mary's been telling me all about your experiences in Africa. I had no idea you'd worked in Olduvai Gorge. And with the famous Leakeys, I understand. How fascinating!"

"Yes, I was very lucky to get that assignment," I said.

"I can only imagine," he said. "Anyway, I've been wondering what you've decided about joining the field crew this summer."

"First I'd like to ask you some questions," I said.

"Of course."

"What would you say would be the percentage of time I'd spend digging versus cooking and cleaning?" I asked.

"Oh, I don't know," he replied. "Maybe sixty-forty?"

I narrowed my eyes. "How about eighty-twenty? And everyone makes their own lunch?"

He thought for a moment. "I guess that would be okay."

I continued. "And I was wondering if you could hire someone else to do the grocery shopping. I'd be willing to give up whatever money you were going to pay me to do that."

Wally smiled. "Ah, negotiation."

"Yes," I said. "Negotiation. I'd like to take the job, but I want to be home on Saturdays."

Mary walked up behind Wally and settled her hands on his shoulders. He leaned back against her, his hands on the top of his crutches. She spoke. "I could do the grocery shopping for the crew each week. If you gave me a list."

He looked up at her. "Are you sure? It would be every week for the entire summer."

She nodded. "Absolutely. Henrietta could leave a list for me on Fridays, and I'd shop on Saturdays and leave the groceries in the lab."

"That would be perfect," I said. "Thanks, Mary. Mr. Whitehurst, is that all right with you?"

"Sure, I guess that would be fine."

I took a big inhale, my heart fluttering. "Then my answer is yes, I'd like the job."

"Excellent!" he said, a big grin blooming across his face. "So you're up for wilderness camping? In addition to the cooking and digging?"

Mary slapped one of his shoulders. "Wally, stop. Are you trying to talk her out of it?"

He reached up and patted her hand.

"You mean digging and cooking, right? In that order? I'm experienced with wilderness camping, so that won't be a problem." The bead of excitement grew inside me. "And there won't be any cheetahs or lions or black mambas, so it should be less deadly than camping in Africa."

"That's settled, then," Mr. Whitehurst said. "I'll go ahead and let Dr. Small know. And Hans, of course."

Oh, joy of joys. I'd almost forgotten that Hans was going. I'd better pack my snake repellent after all.

Kima's dark eyes widened and the lines framing them deepened. "You're doing *what*?" she demanded.

"I'm going on a dinosaur dig in the badlands," I repeated, turning my head at her in puzzlement as I set my stack of returns on the desk. "So I'll need some books to take with me." Commuting to Dickerson every weekday had limited my opportunities to visit the bookstore. I had finally hit upon a Saturday when it was open.

Her mouth was a tight bow. "You're going to dig in the badlands?" "Yes, as soon as the weather clears," I said. "Is something wrong?" She exhaled out of her nostrils like a bull, stood with hands on her hips, and glared at me. "The badlands are sacred to my people. Many of my people were sacrificed there. You should not be digging in the sacred land."

"But I won't be digging for bones of people," I tried to clarify. "I'll be digging for bones of dinosaurs." I gazed back at her, uncomprehending.

"The badlands are one of the places where we reach the Creator. Many spirit guides live there. Mysterious acts happen in the badlands. It is not a place to take lightly."

"I promise not to take it lightly. Being there, I mean." I paused. "You know, someone told me that native peoples' religion includes reverence for the land. Is that true? Wouldn't finding treasures to share be part of that?"

Kima stared into my eyes for a moment, her expression darkening. "The Creator is in all things—the land, the mountains, the animals, the people. No one can truly know the Creator unless they understand this."

She turned without further comment and retreated to the back room of her store. She certainly seemed unsettled, I thought. I loved rocks and fossils, but I didn't think they were imbided with any kind of spirit. The concept was hard for me to imagine.

I meandered over to the shelves and began to look at the titles. Maybe some science fiction? The badlands might be just the place to read about aliens, with all that big sky and wide-open space.

Distracted, I stepped back and bumped right into Kima, who appeared again, suddenly behind me. I turned to face her.

"Here," she said, shoving a book in my hands. "Read this."

I held out my hands and accepted the book. *Silent Spring* by Rachel Carson.

"What does this have to do with the badlands?" I asked, puzzled.

"Nothing. And everything," Kima said, cryptically.

I studied the cover. I guess the aliens would have to wait.

CHAPTER 18

Thank the good Lord, by late April, morning temperatures crossed above the freezing mark. By then, it seemed that the general populace considered the temperature irrelevant. North Dakotans decided winter was over, emerging from their homes in short sleeves to breathe in the fresh spring air. While I was still bundled in my coat, our neighbors tossed theirs into the back of their closets.

With snow squalls over and driving less hazardous, I settled into a weekly routine. On Fridays I dropped Frank at work, leaving the museum early to do my grocery shopping, and picking him up at the end of his workday. One late afternoon, I pulled our station wagon, laden with Dakota Save Rite bags, into Monroe Petroleum's parking lot. I was early. Turning off the engine, I cranked open my side window, letting the spring air settle around me. As I reached for a book to fill my time, I noticed the company's front door opening. Who should appear but Faye Monroe.

Faye stood out against the gray building like a beacon on a dark night. The blue headband across her platinum-blonde flip perfectly matched the trim on her herringbone pantsuit. Her eyes searched the parking lot. Unsure if she saw me, I raised a tentative hand to wave through my windshield. She spied me, a smile forming across her face. Her cowboy-booted feet strode over to my open window.

She leaned down and rested one forearm against my car. "Hello! Henrietta, right?" she asked.

Her memory again floored me. I had not seen her since the Christmas party. "Hello, Faye. It's been a long time. I wasn't sure you'd remember me."

She waved a hand as if swatting a fly. "Of course I do. How did you fare this winter? It was a long one."

I shared her smile. "Yes, it was. But I ended up working at the museum, in the paleo lab. And I have you to thank for that. For introducing me to Wally Whitehurst at your Christmas party."

"Oh, I'm glad that worked out for you. Wally's a dear, special friend."

"What about you?" I asked. "Have you been busy with your column?"

"Oh yes. Some people might think my column is just fluff, but I'll tell you, it takes a lot more effort than anyone knows. It's not all parties and events. I have to remember who is related to whom, who's speaking to each other, and who's on the outs. Fortunately, I have a good memory," she said, tapping her temple. Her eyes revealed a glint of steel behind her beauty queen exterior.

I replied, "I would be terrible at that. Social situations aren't my thing."

She laughed. "Yes, as I recall your thing is to 'dig stuff up.'"

"That's right! I'll be going out into the badlands with the museum's field crew this summer to dig for dinosaurs."

The sun glanced off her teeth. "Well, that sounds exciting. Good for you!"

"Yes, I think it will be," I said. "You know, I think of you when I walk down the museum hall with the Indian artifacts. It doesn't compare to the display in your entry foyer."

"Oh, yes, that's one of my collections. I'm like a magpie. I love shiny, unique things. Fortunately, George puts up with my passions."

"Did you always collect artifacts? I began collecting fossils when I was a kid," I said, my heart warming at the memory.

I detected a falter in her smile. "Not as a child, no. I started later."

"Aren't you from North Dakota? It seems like there are a lot of artifacts spread around the state."

The lines on her forehead accentuated. "There wasn't any time for collecting when I was growing up. I'm from a tiny farming town north of here. I didn't come from much, I'll tell you that. But I did okay. Landed on my feet, shall we say."

"You certainly did. You have a beautiful home, that's for sure," I said.

She bit her lower lip and continued, looking past me. "When you grow up like I did, you'll do anything to keep your treasures around you. George may not be the easiest man to live with, but you could say he's my knight in shining armor."

Then she blushed and cleared her throat, summoning once again her perky voice. "Here I am going on and on. I've gotta run. It was good to see you, Henrietta."

She straightened and, with a backward wave, continued along the line of parked cars, climbing into a cherry-red Mustang. As I watched her peel out of the lot, I considered the many compromises of women.

By early May, the mercury touched the sixties on sunny afternoons. Spring, as I knew it, had fully arrived, and she had taken her sweet time. Hallelujah. The field season would soon begin, and preparations were underway.

"Hey, Hen," Hans said to me from the door of the lab, "want to help me at the barn now that you're on the payroll?"

I narrowed my eyes as I slid my chair away from my prep room workspace. "Sure, as long as you stop calling me 'Hen.' I'm not a chicken."

He offered his infuriating grin as bile rose in my gut.

I grabbed my jacket from the coat cabinet and followed him outside. The sun's rays splashed across my face as I lifted my chin toward the sky and inhaled deeply. I couldn't help cracking a smile, even with the present company. We climbed into the museum's pickup, a secondhand beater someone had donated. Hans put the truck into gear and drove east, past any vestiges of town.

"Did Whitehurst give you a key to the museum?" he asked.

"Yes, *Mr.* Whitehurst gave me one," I said, emphasizing the "mister."

This comment only made him smile wider.

"Did he go over your job responsibilities?"

"Somewhat," I said. "He said I'd be digging for eighty percent of the time and cooking for twenty percent."

"Oh really? That's news to me." He smirked. "I heard you palmed off the grocery shopping to Mary."

"I negotiated. Not 'palmed it off.'"

"Well, here's the drill. *Mr.* Whitehurst will tell you the budget and give Mary cash each week for the groceries. You'll leave a list for her in the lab when we get back each Friday. Make sure the list includes all our food, as well as paper stuff like toilet paper, and charcoal briquettes. There's no wood in the field, so if we want to have a fire, we'll need the briquettes."

I turned and looked at him. "Am I cooking on charcoal every night?"

"No, no." He shook his head, turning off a paved road onto a gravel track. "We have a propane camp stove. But the smoke from the briquettes keeps down the bugs. Anyway, Mary will leave the groceries in the prep lab. She'll put anything that needs to be kept cold in the fridge, and you can transfer that stuff into the big cooler on Monday mornings."

"Do I need to make ice for the cooler?"

"Oh yeah, I almost forgot that. On Fridays, be sure to fill a big container with water and stick it in the freezer so we have a block of ice on Monday for the cooler. Only plan for food to stay cold for a couple of days. After the ice melts, we'll have to eat canned or boxed food."

"Sounds easy enough, as long as everyone isn't too picky."

We rode along in silence for a few miles, the town behind us, grassland extending as far as I could see. I stared out the side window. The monotonous landscape offered feelings of peace as well as desolation.

I turned back toward Hans. "So what's your story?" I asked. "How did you come to work at the museum?"

He looked genuinely surprised. "You mean, my life's path?"

"Yeah."

He glanced over toward me for an instant, then returned his vision to the road. "I've got five sisters," he said. "There was no money for college, but I worked my way through to get my bachelor's. This job opened up, and I took it right out of school. Been here ever since. That's pretty much it."

"Are you the oldest?"

He tapped the steering wheel with his fingers. "Nope, I'm sandwiched in the middle."

"Did your sisters torture you or something?"

His head pulled back in surprise. "What? No. Why would you ask that?"

I shrugged. "Just testing a hypothesis. Did you grow up in North Dakota? Your accent sounds like you did."

"Yep, from Fargo."

"Ever think of going somewhere else? Seeing more of the world?"

He snorted. "Every damn day, Hen. Every damn day."

With that, he reached over and clicked the radio on. Conversation closed. The Turtles crooned "Happy Together" over the airwaves. I laughed to myself. If I were looking for a song that was diametrically opposed to our relationship, I couldn't have done a better job.

A solitary white clapboard farmhouse appeared out of nowhere, its exterior paint faded and chipped. We drove past without slowing. "Where are we?" I asked. "Does someone live in that house?"

"We're almost at the barn. See it down there?" Hans pointed out the windshield. "I think the house is abandoned, but we rent the storage barn from the owners." In the distance along the lane, an old barn came into view. "That's our warehouse, so to speak," Hans said. Arriving, we pulled into the dirt area out front. The barn looked in better shape than the house, which was not saying much. Originally painted red, the wooden slats were weathered, and several needed replacing. Reaching two stories, the rusted metal roof peaked on the right-hand side like a steeple. The building was asymmetrical, the left side once being accessed by double barn doors, I assumed. These had been replaced by a massive steel roller door. A single door with a tiny window served as the front entry to the structure. Stacks of wooden pallets and lumber were strewn around the front. Several fifty-five-gallon drums rusted next to the pallets. The exterior was overgrown with tall grass, giving the scene an air of neglect.

We climbed out of the truck and walked toward the front. "Ladies first," Hans said with a gallant wave of his hand.

I climbed up the cinder-block steps to the front door, and my face was immediately engulfed in a maze of spiderwebs. I flailed my hands, pulling at the strands, and stepped quickly back down. "Yuck, spiders!"

Hans chuckled. "Oh, sorry about that. I forgot the spiders are attracted to this light." He pointed to a bare bulb next to the door. Jangling keys on a ring, he unlocked the door, shoved it open, and stepped around me.

Still swiping at webs, I followed him into the interior and squinted in the gloom. Hans flipped a switch on the wall, and light flooded the barn. I stood back and took in the view.

The floor was hard-packed dirt. The garage bay on the left was empty except for a forklift and several stacks of pallets. An aisle had been cleared lengthwise across the inside of the barn, wide enough for the forklift to maneuver. Along the back wall, irregular shelves had been constructed from mismatched pieces of lumber, drywall, and cinder blocks. The shelves held crates filled with bone-filled blocks of all sizes. Pallets with large jacketed boulders sat in corners.

My eyes widened at this treasure trove. The amount of material in here could keep the lab technicians busy for years.

On my left, a giant steel table containing a rock saw was surrounded by plaster shreds in snowy piles. To the right, canvas tents were stacked haphazardly. Bags of plaster and rolls of burlap splayed in piles. Next to a side door, various sizes of shovels, picks, and sledgehammers leaned against the right-hand wall. The stench of machine oil mixed with the scents of earth, plaster, and moldy canvas.

"Come on, Hen," Hans said. "We need to load up a bunch of these tools. And we'll need to get the stove and the propane tank. I've got to fill the tank this week."

Visions of an accidental natural gas explosion filled my mind with glee as I spit out the last remaining globs of spiderweb.

CHAPTER 19

The first day of fieldwork finally arrived. My heart whipped with elation as my stomach churned with pre-morning coffee and nerves. Muted streaks of sunlight skittered into the museum parking lot as Frank and I pulled in. Two pickup trucks with lowered tailgates were parked by the side door. Hans stood next to a burly middle-aged man who I assumed was Dr. Theo Small. A younger man tossed a crate in the back of one of the trucks.

I took a last sip of coffee from my thermos and exited our station wagon. Frank grabbed my duffel bag and tent from the back seat. As we approached the group, Hans came forward.

"Morning." He waved the older man forward to meet us. "Theo, this is Henrietta Bailey, our cook and chief bottle washer," he said.

"Nice to meet you. I'm Dr. Theo Small," he said. "I hope you can cook." His name was certainly a misnomer. "Small" he was not. Dr. Small had the build of a rhino and a face to match. A smirky grin broke out over his heavily jowled face, which made his large nose even more prominent.

"Since we are using titles, I'm Dr. Henrietta Ballantine," I said, unsmilingly. "And I cannot cook in the least. They didn't cover that in grad school. But I know how to light a camp stove and open a can, so we won't starve. This is my husband, Frank."

Dr. Small turned toward Frank and extended his hand. "Good to meet you. I hear you work for Monroe Petroleum?"

"Yep, I'm oil field trash and proud of it," Frank said, appearing to tighten his grip.

The third man wandered over. "This is Rob Harkness," Dr. Small said. "Rob's a grad student at Dakota State." Rob and Frank shook hands, and Rob nodded to me. He looked to be about my age and was a skinny bunch of kneecaps, elbows, and flappy ears.

"All right, let's load the trucks."

Frank made sure to give me a big public kiss in the parking lot before slamming back into our car. "Be careful, Henrietta. I'll miss you. See you on Friday."

"I'll miss you too," I said, leaning in through the window for a final peck.

And then our field crew took off, driving north on an asphalt road bisecting the prairie, the badlands cropping up in the distance. I rode with Rob in the museum's truck, jostling up and down on the passenger seat, peering out the side window. Clumps of pale green wheatgrass lined the road, sprouting from the sparse regolith as if anxious for rain. The farther we drove the more neglected the pavement. Freeze-thaw had been at work here over the winter, the roadbed alternately contracting and expanding, busting itself apart. The edges crumbled onto the narrow shoulder.

"Were you part of last year's crew?" I asked.

Rob nodded, his right hand on the wheel, his left elbow resting on the open window. A hot breeze blew into the truck. "Yeah, only at the end of the dig, though. A bunch of grad students rotated in and out. A buddy of mine had to leave early, and I took his spot."

"Is your buddy coming out to dig this summer too?"

"No, he graduated. I think it's just the four of us this summer," Rob said.

"The whole summer?"

He shrugged. "Yeah, just the way Dr. Small scheduled it, I guess."

"And you're studying geology?"

"No. I've taken some geology classes, but I'm studying wildlife biology. Big mammals. I'm specializing in bison. I'm just here to get paid."

"Bison, huh? Are there bison in the badlands?"

"Oh, yeah. The big herds are long gone, but we might run across a few. You need to keep your distance from them, though. They can be nasty. Especially if they have calves."

"I'll remember that if I see any," I said, remembering the wildebeest in Africa.

After an hour, we turned off road, following Theo and Hans onto a dirt track marked by no discernable marker I could fathom. We bounced down a dry gully, and Rob shifted gears to climb up the other side.

"This is all BLM land," he said, waving his hand to indicate the plain and the approaching ridges.

I felt my brow crease with concern. I replied, "I thought we weren't allowed to dig on BLM land."

"We're allowed to dig because the museum has a permit. Otherwise, no, you're not."

As our caravan of two hurdled closer to our destination, the landscape changed, and the dissected hills of the badlands came into sharper focus. The softly eroded slopes resembling melted candlewax, exposed their horizontal stripes of strata. The rocks here seemed darker in color than where Frank and I usually hiked, more russet and mahogany rather than ivory and beige. The mounds were lower in elevation. Vertical runnels dug into the sides of the hills as if scratched by the claws of a gigantic beast. Pencil-like hoodoos stood like lonely sentinels, covered in resistant caprock.

Any semblance of the dirt track vanished, and we turned to drive across the sagebrush. I clutched the edge of my seat as our truck vaulted over grass clumps and skirted around boulders. My stomach tumbled. Rob pointed through the windshield at a rounded hill in the distance. "That's where we're headed."

In the west, the sky began to turn a slaty gray. A thickening cumulonimbus cloud grew like a sinister, convoluted creature. Its darkening base hovered in a horizontal plane at the condensation level, mirroring the peaks in an inverted arrangement.

Theo and Hans stopped in front of an arcuate hill towering over our heads in front of us. Alluvium aggregated in talus cones along its base. Sporadic juniper trees clung to life along the weathered slopes.

We pulled up parallel to their truck and stepped out, the kicked-up dust settling around us.

Theo walked over to us. "Well, this is it. Home sweet home. Last year we had our tents over there. You can see the remains of the firepit." He folded his arms. "Keep a lookout for rattlesnakes. They love to hide under the sagebrush."

We lowered the tailgates and began to unpack. I hefted my rolled-up canvas pup tent and dragged it through grassy patches near the firepit. Finding a relatively smooth spot on the ground, I dropped my tent and turned to retrieve my duffel bag. Hans walked up to me and held out a shovel.

"First-time field crew members get to dig the latrine. That means you. Over there, at least a hundred feet away." He smiled his pompous grin and pointed.

A slow burn started behind my eyes. I wrenched the shovel out of his hand and glared at him, my mouth set in a straight line. "I'll be happy to start the digging. But everybody can take a turn. Otherwise, I won't be able to bother with cooking our dinner."

Hans's eyes widened at my tone. Rob walked between us and reached out his hand for the shovel. "I'll start the latrine hole," he said. "And Henrietta's right. We can all help dig." He looked over at me. "We even have a wooden seat this year. And a tarp and poles to set up around the hole. For privacy."

Ah, such luxury.

—•—

Last summer's digging efforts had left a bowl-like depression at the base of the hillside. The excavation was covered with loose rock, purposely placed there at the end of the summer to protect the site from the winter's blast of snow and wind. Our first job was to remove the debris and uncover the site. Then the dig could start where it had left off.

Shovels clanged through the piles of loose debris. Our campsite being just a stone's throw from the excavation, the scent of breakfast still hung in the air. I had managed to fry sausage and mix it with scrambled eggs, although the meat had stuck viciously to the bottom of the pan. No one complained about the charred bits. I counted that as a small victory. The fresh food in the cooler would not last long, I knew.

No storm had materialized overnight, and today we were blessed with clear blue skies. A hawk circled above us on a thermal as the ground began to heat from the sun. I pulled my hat down to shade my face and rested a moment, leaning on my shovel.

"Don't stop now. We've only just begun," Hans prodded as he tossed a shovel full of debris sideways into a pile.

Even he could not dampen my mood. I ignored him and turned to Theo. "Dr. Small, can you tell me about the geology here?"

He looked up, surprise on his face. "Sure. I don't know how much you know, but this is all Hell Creek Formation. Late Cretaceous in age. We're at what was once a low-lying coast on the edge of the Western Interior Seaway, which stretched from the Gulf of Mexico to the Arctic and split the continent into two halves. The sandstones and mudstones of Hell Creek were deposited by streams, in flood-plains and swamps. Of course, dinosaurs walked all over this area. Crocodiles have been found here too, so we know the paleoclimate was subtropical."

"Mr. Whitehurst said this site might have been where bones once collected along a bend in a river. Like along a point bar?"

"Exactly. There are parts of several species here. Preservation is not great. Last year we jacketed a few bones and brought them to the storage barn. They're probably from either a hadrosaur or a ceratopsid."

"What about vegetation?" I asked. "Have you found any plant fossils?"

"Yes, you'll see the organic remains of leaves and twigs all over the place," he said, waving his arm. "You can find them in pieces of float on the ground."

"Maybe I could take some samples for pollen analysis? I studied palynology in grad school."

"Sure. Help yourself."

Digging continued until lunchtime. Bologna sandwiches and chips. Then back to the shovels. The temperature hovered around eighty degrees. Sweat beaded inside my shirt. I wiped my brow with my work glove. My biceps, not used to manual labor, ached, and my knees complained from the stooping. I soldiered on, determined not to show any weakness.

By day's end, I held my breath as the last of the loose debris was removed from the site. I looked down, expecting to see bones appear, disentombed from their wintery grave. But nothing stood out as bone, at least to my eyes.

Dr. Small knelt on the ground. "See here? That's the edge of a bone."

I studied the surface and frowned. "Hmm . . . it all looks the same to me."

"Look right here." He pointed at the surface. "See the texture difference?"

I lowered to my knees beside him and looked where he was pointing. "Not really, no."

"Run your finger over it, from here to here," he said.

I did as he suggested, letting my finger traverse across the rock. "Maybe a little difference. Nothing I'd pick out on my own, though."

"Spit on it," Hans said.

"What?"

"Jeez, girlie girl. Spit on it. Or does that disgust you?"

There certainly was something that disgusted me, but it was not spit. Although I was somewhat dehydrated, I managed to lean over and spit on the rock. I rubbed my saliva into the ground with my pointer finger. A tiny, barely noticeable change in color appeared between rock and bone.

"Ah, yes, I see it now," I said. "Fascinating."

"Okay, Mr. Spock," Hans muttered under his breath.

If only someone would beam *him* up.

CHAPTER 20

My palms blistered and my knees were scraped and covered in Band-Aids. For two weeks I had been relegated to trenching far from the bones so they could be removed within large blocks of rock. In addition to my cooking and cleaning chores, of course. Digging was digging, though, and at least I was a part of it.

At day's end, the sun tucked behind the buttes and washed the top spires with a red-orange hue as if brushed by God's hand. Our dinner of fried potatoes and Vienna sausages filled our bellies, another lackluster meal checked off my list. I scraped and wiped the pots and stored the food away for the night.

A fire flared in the pit, fueled by charcoal briquettes. Their chemical stink coated the air and turned my stomach. The three men lounged on flat rocks, slurping warm beer from cans. I joined them, carrying a marshmallow poked on a flattened metal coat hanger. Extending it into the fire, it caught, flaring in the semidarkness like my own personal torchlight. I brought it toward me and blew out the flames. After waiting a moment for it to cool, I took a cautious bite. The sticky goo hit my tongue with just the right mixture of molten sugar and burnt bits.

"How's the marshmallow?" Hans asked.

"Delicious," I said. "Want one?"

"No, thanks," he said, turning up his nose. "I'm not a ten-year-old Girl Scout."

I ignored him and took another bite. The hoot of an owl carried on the breeze from its distant lair.

Theo cleared his throat. "You know, now that we've shoveled off the loose debris, I've had a fresh look at the bones we left in the ground. Overall, I just don't think the preservation is great. Last year, the bones we extracted were disarticulated or crushed. I haven't seen anything so far to indicate these will be any better."

"That's a shame," Rob said. "I hope this won't be a waste of a field season."

"It's only been two weeks," I said. "You can't tell already, can you?"

"No, but I don't want to get anyone's hopes up," Theo said. "So far I can't even tell if the remaining bones belong to a lizard-hipped saurischian or a bird-hipped ornithischian."

"It might be another hadrosaur." Hans faced me. "That's a duck-billed dinosaur."

"I know what a hadrosaur is," I replied. "Are duck-bills common in the Hell Creek Formation, Dr. Small?"

He nodded. "Yes, pretty common. You know, John Ostrom thinks some dinosaurs may have traveled in herds."

"I've heard of John Ostrom. From Yale," I said. (*Thank you, Dad.*)

"A great man. I studied under him," Theo said, a pretentious note in his voice. He cleared his throat. "Anyway, that might be why hadrosaurs are so common . . . there may have been herds of them."

"I know the museum already has one hadrosaur skeleton—an *Edmontosaurus*," I said.

Hans slurped his beer. "We have several."

"I'm not sure these bones will be worth bringing in, considering the transportation costs," Theo said. "I guess we'll have to see."

This mantra rang hollow in my ears. The bones had looked intact to me. But what did I know? And how did Theo know, when only the edges were visible? The rest were still embedded in rock.

The rims of the charcoal briquettes began to whiten as the sky changed from dusk to darkness, the sun giving its last gasp as if exhausted from its day. Hans pulled out a harmonica and placed it to his lips. The low, mournful notes of "The Sound of Silence" wafted out. I sat in awe, having no notion that Hans could play the harmonica. The final chord floated up into the troposphere with the invisibility of water vapor.

"Wow," I said. "That was beautiful."

Hans replied. "Thanks, Hen." Then he took a last gulp of his beer, crushed the can against his rock seat, and flung the flattened metal into the briquettes. He followed the motion with a loud belch.

Pursing my lips, I stared straight up into the indigo sky. A bat flitted overhead, diving after a bug with its silent echolocation.

I rose to my feet. "I'm going to bed. See you *gentlemen* in the morning."

CHAPTER 21

Aggravating behavior notwithstanding, I woke up each morning with the same thrill and excitement as on the first day. Four poles held a tarp aloft over us, providing shade from the sun's high-angled summer rays. An afternoon breeze kicked up loose grit, and I pressed my glasses closer against my face. The wind was a double-edged sword, swirling dirt in our eyes and nostrils yet helping to keep us cool and sweeping the mosquitoes away.

How could a desert have this many mosquitoes anyway? I wondered. They were a constant menace.

With four weeks of experience under my belt, I was now allowed to chisel and hammer closer to the bones, and they began to reveal their shapes. I chipped off a large shard of overburden. "Wow," I said. "Look at that!" I set down my hammer and chisel and ran my hand over a newly exposed edge of bone. Wonder filled my brain. I observed its length and curvature. "This one looks like a femur. And a big one too!"

Rob stopped working and leaned over toward me. He shrugged. "Looks big, I'll give you that."

I pointed at the bone he was working on. "And look at the length of that caudal bone." I looked up and smiled at the crew. "This is fantastic!"

Utter shock appeared on Theo's face. It was priceless.

"Do . . . you . . . know dinosaur bone structure?" he stuttered, his eyes widening.

"A little. I spent a lot of time looking at the dinosaur skeletons at the Smithsonian. I'm no expert, though," I said, shrugging.

With the sun in my eyes I could not be sure, but it seemed to me that a disquieted look passed between Theo and Hans.

That evening, I dragged my tired body over to my tent, unzipped the front flap, and crawled inside. Removing my boots, I stuffed them with my socks to prevent anything from crawling inside. Not that I saw any critters in my tent, but you never knew. I zipped the canvas flap halfway up from the bottom, slipped out of my jeans and into my pajama pants, and pulled open my sleeping bag. From my peephole through the top of the flap, I stared out at the twilight just in time to view a meteor streaking across the sky, a vaporizing fragment of space dust.

I missed Frank. Was he thinking of me? I knew he was unhappy with me being out in the field all summer. I would never hear the end of it if we failed to bring back a dinosaur skeleton.

The sky darkened to a deep cerulean, and one by one, the stars birthed in the heavens. The same pulsing beacons had called to the ancients, to the tribes that had once roamed across this land. The Big Dipper shone high above the horizon, set within the Great Bear, Ursa Major. Hercules rested at my zenith, and the bright star Arcturus lit the skyline, anchoring Boötes, the Herdsman. How had the Mandan or Hidatsa tribes described these patterns? Perhaps I would ask Kima when I saw her again. The last few times I had gone to the bookstore, it had been locked up tight.

The scent of marijuana reached me in my tent. I could see the flared end of the rolled joint in the dark as Hans passed it across the fire circle to Theo. Fragments of the men's conversation drifted my way.

Rob: "Not my scene, man."

Hans: ". . . cool, man . . ."

More flaring, like pulsing fireflies in the moonlight. Exhales of smoke. Quiet coughs.

Theo: ". . . before the skull becomes visible . . ."
Hans: ". . . paydirt . . ."
Rob: ". . . distract her with something?"
Theo: ". . . got an idea . . ."
What did that all mean? The words were verbal hieroglyphics, beyond my interpretation. Through the unzipped gap in my tent, the dusty swath of the Milky Way revealed itself, like an unknowable celestial sign across the firmament.

The next morning's sun bloomed as a vermilion orb in a clear sapphire sky. After dressing in my tent and inspecting my boots for inhabitants, I lit the camp stove to make the morning coffee. Filling my tin cup, I leaned against the tailgate, gulping the brew to clear my head. As usual, the coffee held little in the realm of flavor but provided a caffeine jolt nonetheless.

Theo stepped out of his tent, clomped over, and poured himself a cup.

"I'm going to start breakfast in a minute," I said, savoring another gulp.

He squinted into the rising sun. "You know, we're just going to be trenching today. I've got another site I'd like to show you. We found it last year, and you might be just the person to work on it."

"I don't mind digging a trench," I said, even as my muscles protested the white lie.

"The location has plant fossils. Last year I pulled out a bunch of leaf imprints. I figured since you're a paleobotanist . . ."

"Okay. I wouldn't mind taking a look."

"Let's be sure to take the walkie-talkies. We'll be out of sight," Theo said.

We set out after breakfast, walkie-talkies tested and clipped to our knapsacks. The day's heat began to press down through the windless air. Our boots kicked across the clay-rich soil, through the

Indian ricegrass dotting the arid landscape. An occasional yucca took root between the hills, spiny fronds piercing the sky.

"So you went to Yale, huh?" I asked Theo.

He nodded. "Yep. For my doctorate."

"Are you from Connecticut?"

"I am," he said, taking small gasps of breath. "But I headed west a long time ago."

His body type was not built for hiking, I noted. "No dinosaurs in Connecticut, I guess?"

"Actually, did you know that over two thousand dinosaur footprints were discovered in Connecticut last year?"

"Really? No, I didn't."

"Yep, when they were excavating for a new state building. But this is where the bones are, so this is where I ended up," he said.

A sudden burst of wings almost under our feet brought us to a halt. My blood raced as plumage fluttered and flapped at eye level. Instinctively, my hands rose to shield my face from the onslaught. The bird took flight away from us, flashing its white underwings and contrasting ebony belly.

"Jeez, that scared me," I said, placing a hand on my chest as my heart missed a beat. "That was a sage grouse. A female one."

The grouse disappeared into the distant sky.

I continued. "You can tell by her white feathers. They eat those black sagebrush leaves. *Artemisia nova*." I pointed at the plant.

Theo grunted and dabbed his sweaty forehead with his sleeve. "If you say so."

We arrived at a distant badlands hummock, and I turned to look behind us. Our base camp appeared dollhouse-size in the distance.

"The site's down here aways," Theo said. As we rounded the hill, our camp disappeared from sight. We walked along the base, with the cliff face on our left, and I eyeballed the rocks alongside me—the bedded blue-gray marls and peaty clays of the Hell Creek Formation. Theo trudged along the hillside in front of me, breathing heavily. I followed, scanning up and down the strata as I had been taught in Africa when I worked at Olduvai Gorge.

"See that bedding plane there?" Theo stuck his finger on a layer right above my head. "That's a paleosol. A buried soil horizon. I found some plant fossils along this zone last year. Come down this way."

We walked farther along to a spot where the hill had been deeply gouged along the paleosol horizon. "I dug some blocks out from here, and they contained leaf impressions. And permineralized wood."

"What type of leaves?" I asked.

"Heck if I know. They looked like oak leaves to me," he said, shrugging.

"Probably not. Maybe angiosperms of some type, though."

Theo knelt and reached for a weathered brown mudstone from a rubble pile at our feet. "It looks like these fell out over the winter. We might be able to split them and find some plants."

I set down my knapsack and reached inside for my rock hammer. Grabbing one of the rocks, I anchored it between my boots and gave it a solid whack with the hammer. The rock cleaved along a bedding plane. I pulled the halves apart, exposing a dentate leaf, impressed on both sides of the slab. Carbonized bits of bark glittered with streaks of pyrite. A huge smile spread across my face. I remembered my dad's words about "dinosaurs being flashy . . . but other things lived in the Cretaceous too." And here was a site containing my specialty—plant fossils! I could do some actual research here, not just dig up dinosaurs for someone else to study.

"This could keep me busy for the rest of the summer!" I said, waving toward the hill.

"Have at it," Theo said. He unclipped the walkie-talkie from his knapsack and handed it to me. "Let's test this to make sure you're in range."

I toggled on the switch. Static coursed through the air. I pressed the transmitter and held it down.

Squawk!

"Testing, one, two. Can you hear me?"

Screech!

"Affirmative. I can hear you." It was Rob's voice. "Can you hear me?"

"Yes. Affirmative. I'm going to stay at the site for the rest of the day."

"Affirmative. Will leave this switched on."

I released the transmitter and turned to Theo. "Will the museum's permit cover this location? I don't want to dig illegally."

Theo nodded. "Oh, yeah, it will. The site's all yours."

———

For the next few days, a growing pile of plant fossils captivated me. Leaf impressions, carbonized wood, and pyritized bits of bark. I studied each with my hand lens, made sketches, and wrote in my field notebook. At the end of each day, I wrapped specimens in paleo paper, otherwise known as toilet paper. I numbered them, filled my knapsack, and carried them back to base camp.

Each evening, as I approached the camp, the men pulled tarps over the dinosaur excavation. I could see them rolling heavy rocks along the edges of the tarps to anchor them.

None of the men expressed much interest in my plant findings when I unwrapped them.

"Far out," Rob muttered, barely glancing at them.

"Keep at it," said Theo.

"Plant scraps," sniffed Horrible Hans.

———

Our two field trucks pulled into the museum lot, later than usual that Friday. The sun lowered toward the western horizon and the temperature had dropped, adding a slight chill to the air. I could see Frank reclining in the driver's seat of our station wagon, parked along the side. His arms were folded over his chest, and his eyes appeared closed.

I jumped out of the truck and headed over to him. His eyes opened at my approach. He turned his head and glared at me, frowned, and looked pointedly at his watch.

"Hi, honey," I said through the window glass. "I'm sorry we're so late. We got behind with the packing."

In truth, I had lost track of time at my site, hiking back to camp late. Another reason for the chill in the air.

Frank rolled down the window. I started to lean in to kiss him but was stopped by the look on his face.

"Get your stuff and let's go," he said, his eyes stony.

I pulled back. "I've got to fill a water jug to make ice for Monday."

"Hurry up."

I walked back to the pickup and pulled out my duffel and knapsack. Rob was unloading a crate with our field-cleaned pots and pans. "Everything okay?" he asked.

"Sure," I said, turning away. I carried my belongings to our car, swung open the tailgate, and tossed them inside. Rob carried the crate of pans over and slid it next to my duffel. I would wash them at home over the weekend.

"I'll be right back," I called over the seat to Frank, who stared ahead, not moving.

Theo dragged the bags containing our weekly accumulation of garbage across the lot. Cans and bottles clanked inside as he manhandled the bags into a trash can. Hans stood in the bed of the second truck. I hurried over.

"Hans, I need one of those empty water jugs to fill and put in the freezer," I said.

He flicked the hair out of his face. "Hang on." He looked over at Frank in our car and smirked. "It might take me a few minutes."

"I need it. Now," I said, sending poison through my eyes.

He plopped the empty water jugs on the ground. "You know, we're late because of you. Don't forget that."

I picked up one of the jugs and headed to the other truck's bed for my plant fossils. I wanted to take them home and examine them over the weekend.

"I'll get that for you, Henrietta," Rob said, taking the jug out of my hands. "I can fill it and shove it in the freezer. You go ahead and take off."

"Thanks, Rob." I picked up the bin containing my plant fossils and carried it to the car.

Hans appeared next to me. "Don't forget the grocery list. I hope you'll ask for something tasty for a change."

With thoughts of slugging him in his sarcastic face, which is what I wanted to do with every fiber of my being, I pushed the bin into the car and took the list out of my pocket. "Here," I said, shoving it at him. "Can you please put this in the lab for Mary?"

I banged our tailgate shut and walked to the passenger door without waiting for a reply. Frank started the ignition before I reached the door handle and jammed the car into gear as I hit the seat.

Wordlessly, we pulled out of the lot.

The hum of the engine did nothing to dissipate the wretched silence between us. We were quiet for a full twenty minutes before I attempted to speak. "I'm sorry we were so late."

"What the hell, Henrietta?" Frank exploded. "I was waiting there for three hours!"

"It took us a long time to pack."

I snuck a glance at him. The edges of his mouth were down-turned in a deep frown.

"What did Hans mean when he said it was your fault?" he asked.

I swallowed. "I was late coming back to camp this afternoon. I started on a new site this week. With fossil plants. But it's away from the base camp."

"What? You mean you aren't even working on dinosaurs?"

"No. But I think this site will yield some exciting results. There are varieties of angiosperms and pines. I even found a fossilized pine cone. I can do real research, honey. And maybe publish. I brought them home for us to look at. I thought you'd like to see them."

This made no discernable dent in his mood.

"You're at this site by yourself?" he asked.

"Well, yeah. Theo . . . Dr. Small . . . took me there, so he knows where I am."

"How far away is it?"

"What?" I crinkled my eyes at him.

"The new site. Can they see you from the dinosaur dig?"

"No, it's across the plain. And around a hill."

His knuckles whitened as he gripped the steering wheel tighter.

"What if something happens? In an emergency?"

"Oh, I've got a walkie-talkie. I can call on that."

Frank glanced over at me, his eyes catching mine. Then he focused back on the road. "I don't like the idea of you being out of sight, by yourself. Walkie-talkie or not. I don't like it one bit."

I frowned back at him and crossed my arms across my chest. "I'll be fine," I replied in a huff. "I can take care of myself."

Compromises churned through my brain as the ginger-striped sky dimmed into evening purples. The first star of twilight appeared in the heavens like a genie. Goose bumps rose on my arms, and I cranked my window closed, cutting off the breeze.

I turned to Frank. "How about this? I'll ask Mr. Whitehurst if I can use the phone in his office to call you at work when I get to the museum. That way, you can just work late and you won't have to wait for me in the parking lot on Fridays. I can call Mary this weekend and ask her to ask him for me."

"You have a key to his office?" he asked.

"No," I admitted. "But Hans might. If he does, he could let me in."

"I'd think the last thing you'd want to do is ask Hans for a favor," he said.

"But I would. If you wanted to just wait at Monroe for me to call."

Frank sighed deeply and stared ahead. His face, in profile, appeared like carved granite. Tiny lines wearied the edges of his eyes.

He replied, "To be honest, the last thing I want to do is stay longer at my desk. I thought this job would be like my job at National

Bitumen, where my work and opinions were valued. But at Monroe, I can't seem to make any headway."

"You're still upset that your prospect was farmed out, I guess?"

He nodded. "It's not just that. But that sure didn't help. I have a lot of experience, but here I'm treated like a rookie. It's like starting over from scratch."

I slid next to him and reached over to brush a strand of hair off his forehead. He needed a haircut, I noticed. "How is your well doing?" I asked. "Any news?"

"It's drilling. I get reports from Warhawk's geologist. They dropped a tool down the hole and had to fish for most of this week. That slowed them down."

"I have no idea what that means, but it sounds bad."

"Yeah, it was bad. And costly, but of course it's their money. They're back to drilling now. Schlumberger should be logging in a couple of weeks."

Our headlights finally illuminated the town limits of Mammoth. The red neon sign in front of Clara's flickered in the dark, with half of its letters burned out. It read CLARA BA & GR.

I pointed at the sign. "Look. Clara's Bah and Growl."

Frank smiled for the first time, lifting some of the pressure off my chest. "My stomach said that after eating there," he said. "How about Clara's—Get Baked and Groove?"

I chuckled. "I don't think it's that hip. How about Clara's Bra and Garters?"

Frank groaned. "Ugh, I don't want to think about those things in reference to Clara."

"No?"

"No. Not ever." He winked at me as he turned into our street. "But I could think about them in reference to *you*."

The following morning, I unwrapped my plant fossils to show to Frank. Chunks of shale splayed across our kitchen table, and a ream of filthy paleo paper piled on the floor. We sipped our coffee while examining them, slivers of rock escaping onto our laps.

I leaned back in my chair, the luxury of lounging in my pajamas causing all my muscles to feel like warmed honey. The coffee helped. As had our evening activities.

Frank held up a slab containing part of a carbonized leaf. "I don't know what to tell you. To me, this looks like the stuff that didn't turn into coal."

"Yeah, that's right. It isn't coal. Bury it for tens of millions of years, and then it might interest you, huh?"

"Yep, then it might be economical."

"You have to admit that the fossil pine cone is cool," I said.

He picked up the caramel-colored pine cone between two fingers. It was tiny—about an inch long. "I can see the indentations from the scales, but the whole thing is kind of squashed."

"Have you ever seen anything like it in your travels?" I asked.

He swiveled it in the light. "Not that I recall. But honestly, honey, it's not my field."

My stomach began to growl. "Do you want me to make us some breakfast? I now have lots of experience frying Spam. Not that we have any Spam. Or I could make toast."

"No, thanks. I can make toast," he said. "You'd be impressed with how self-sufficient I am now. Not to mention I'd made breakfast on my own for years before you came along."

"Terrific. Can you make some toast for me too?" I asked with a fake flutter of my eyelashes.

Frank pushed off from the table. "Sure. I guess it's my penance for being such a jerk last night."

I let that comment slide by and watched as he unwrapped a loaf of white bread and popped two slices into our toaster. He opened the refrigerator and retrieved the butter dish.

Returning my gaze to my plant fossils, I moved them around on the table. "I wonder if the Cretaceous plants from Hell Creek have been studied extensively by anyone? Or if I could do some new research with these?"

The toast sprung up, the warm scent wafting across the kitchen. Frank slid the pieces onto a plate, buttered them, and set the plate in front of me. "Here you go," he said. "To answer your question—I have no idea. But I bet I know who you could ask to find out."

I looked up at him.

"My dad," I said as he nodded in agreement.

Great minds, and all that.

CHAPTER 22

New plant fossils absorbed all my attention for the next week. Like never-ending birthday gifts, they kept on giving. And I greedily accepted them, each discovery causing my heart to skip, no matter how mundane the leaf or twig.

Late afternoon, my shadow lengthening and the heat pressing down on my back, I rested on the ground at my site. A swig of water from my canteen brought blessed relief to my parched throat. As I drank, my eyes wandered up and down the outcrop, tracing the homogenous beds. Horizontal stripes of olive-gray, ecru, and mahogany shales and siltstones paralleled the peaty paleosol layer. An entire forest had grown in that soil horizon at the edge of the Western Interior Seaway. Conifers, cycads, and ginkgoes had flourished alongside flowering plants and ferns, their roots anchored in the rich soil. Dinosaurs munched on the vegetation or hunted in its shade. In the waters of the nearby seaway, gigantic mosasaurs and long-necked plesiosaurs preyed upon fishes and ammonites. Pterosaurs and diving birds glided overhead.

I contemplated these prehistoric beasts as I packed my knapsack with the day's discoveries. After another full week of digging, cooking, and hauling, exhaustion crept into my body. The weight of the knapsack strained my arms as I hefted it and tugged at my shoulders as I began the slow hike across the prairie to base camp. I realized with a pang that the field season was half over.

A web of mixed emotions crept over me. I loved the thrill of digging at my own site and finding new specimens each day. Would I discover previously undescribed species? The possibility of undertaking this research kept me charging ahead, digging alone in the desert. Yet I was unsure if that would be the case. Had all these plants already been studied? And with the summer half over, the thought of another bitter winter lurking behind the tease of warm weather made me shudder.

My weary feet dragged through the wheatgrass and across the pebbly soil. With my eyes cast downward on the lookout for rattlesnakes, a distinctive object on the ground caught my attention. I stopped and knelt for a better view.

It was an arrowhead.

Composed of milky quartz, the arrowhead glimmered with an opalescence in the sunshine. I picked it up, and its warmth radiated across my palm. Running my thumb down the chipped sides, I felt the sharp edges scrape across my skin.

How long ago had someone hunted with this arrowhead? Who dropped it, here in the middle of nowhere?

The thought struck me. *Maybe I'll show it to Kima.*

I looked around on the ground for others but found none. It was an outlier. Was it rare? I didn't know. Did it have a story? Absolutely. I pocketed the artifact and continued back to the campsite.

The next Friday, when I arrived back home in Mammoth, a thick envelope awaited me.

July 16, 1967

Dear Henrietta,
How wonderful to hear your voice last Sunday—
thank you for calling—your mother especially

appreciated the call. We are looking forward to your trip home in September, and you can visit the museum library then—but I went ahead as you requested and looked for research on Cretaceous flora—most specifically from the Hell Creek Formation. I found several articles published in the Journal of Geology— the most recent one is copied and included here. It seems a researcher with the U. of Montana has done quite a lot of work on the subject. Your pine cone is probably from the genus Metasequoia—which is fairly common according to the paper.

This doesn't mean that more research can't be done, of course. Perhaps you can collaborate.

Your mother sends her love. Our regards to Frank.

Love,
Dad

Saturday morning, I sat on the couch, reading for a third time the enclosed scientific paper titled *Cretaceous Flora of the Hell Creek Formation, North Dakota and Montana.* My dad was correct in that extensive study had already been done on my plant fossils. The bibliography listed numerous other publications on the subject.

Frank leaned over the back of the couch, placing his hands on my shoulders. "Bad news?" he asked.

I shuffled the pages. "Yes and no," I said. "The good news is that a lot of work has been done on Hell Creek plant fossils, so I'll be able to identify them fairly easily."

"Okay..."

"The bad news is that a lot of work has been done on Hell Creek plant fossils..."

"And you were hoping to be the one to do the work," Frank completed the statement for me.

"Yes, exactly," I said, my shoulders sagging.

Frank walked around the couch and plopped down next to me. The cushions sagged under his weight, causing me to tilt against him. He put his arm around me. "Like your dad said, there's always more research to be done."

I nodded. "I know. I'd hoped to identify some new species, though, and look at this list in the paper." I flipped the pages to the taxonomy at the end. "They've identified almost thirty species already."

Frank squeezed my shoulder. "Maybe you can design a new exhibit with the plant fossils. You know, identify them, write an information panel on why they're important. Arrange the exhibit. I'll bet Wally would go for that. The fossils belong to the museum after all."

"Maybe." With a sigh, I reached up and feathered my fingers through the hair overlapping his collar. "In the meantime, you're overdue for a haircut. We can't have you looking like a hippie."

He chuckled. "Probably not the right look for Monroe Petroleum."

"Let's walk into town. I'll bet Tiny could use a customer."

⁂

Outside, the sun lurked behind rows of thick stratocumulus clouds, playing the occasional game of peek-a-boo with our shadows. Perhaps a warm front was approaching. Frank disappeared into Tiny's Barbershop as I passed the striped pole and pushed open the door to the bookstore. The bell jangled above my head. The interior appeared in its usual gloom with no one in sight, so I browsed among the stacks, taking in the familiar musty scent. Once again the haphazard stacking of books niggled at my brain's need for organization. I pulled out a few selections, tucking them into the crook of my left arm.

"Henrietta," Kima said from behind me.

I jumped, goose bumps blooming on my skin. She was as stealthy as a bobcat.

"Kima," I said, turning toward her. "I brought you something. From the badlands."

Reaching into my pocket, my fingers gripped the arrowhead. I pulled it out and offered it to her, flat on my palm. The vitreous luster of the quartz seemed to shine with an otherworldly essence in the shadowed space.

She stared at it.

"It's an arrowhead, right?" I asked.

She waited a beat. "You have to put it back," she said, the edges of her mouth turning down.

"What? Why? I thought you might like to have it. I brought it for you. I didn't dig for it. I picked it up off the ground." I extended my hand out toward her.

She looked directly at me. "Put. It. Back. That is part of my heritage. Do you understand? My culture."

I bit my lip. "You want your culture thrown back on the ground? I don't understand."

"No, you do not." She folded her arms in front of her. "I told you that the badlands are sacred to my people. First, the land was taken away and we were moved to reservations. Then, the bones of our ancestors and our sacred objects were put in museums. In cabinets and boxes. Do you know how painful it is to see those things in museums?"

I swallowed. "No . . ."

"Do you know what happened after that? Oil was discovered on our land. Wells were drilled. Next, there will be pipelines. Did you read *Silent Spring*?"

"By Rachel Carson? Yes."

"Good. Because that's what will happen here next. Not with the same chemicals, but others. They've taken our land. Our water will be next. Fouled. Polluted."

"How do you know?"

"Trust me, I know. My family and I will try to stop these things. Someone must stand up for the land. And it starts with little things like this." She reached out and tapped the arrowhead with her finger.

My face warmed as blood rushed to my cheeks. "I'm sorry. I didn't realize."

"One day, you also will be called upon to protect the land. Perhaps not here. But somewhere sacred."

I was taken aback. "Me? Why me? I'm not part of your family."

She gazed at me for a moment and shook her head. Reaching toward me, she placed her hand firmly on my shoulder. I felt its weight radiate down to my toes. "We are all family. Sisters. Mothers. Daughters." And she gave me a slow smile.

My breath stopped in my throat and my chest tightened. I had heard those same words, a few years before. In Africa. From a woman who I considered to be my guardian angel. Although I had never determined if she was real or an illusion.

The hairs on the back of my neck stood out, electrified. Within the depths of her dark, wise eyes I could glimpse a hint of my future. Then her face closed down, replaced by a silent mask, and she steered me out the door, shutting it behind me with a click.

Outside on the sidewalk, my arms quaked around my clutch of paperbacks. Looking down, it dawned on me that I had not paid Kima for the books. This fact seemed unimportant, like a tiny tremor after a major seismic event.

CHAPTER 23

Parched from the late July aridity, the sagebrush crunched crisply under my boots. My denim pant legs made a scuffing noise as I headed toward my fossil site. I took no comfort in the circling kettle of vultures overhead, usually a harbinger of death. The peeling skin on my nose and arms evidenced my long summer days in the sun, and I pulled the brim of my hat down to cover my face.

Where had I picked up the arrowhead?

I searched for a spot close to its original resting place, remembering a clump of nearby wheatgrass, a fact that had no hope of narrowing down the location. At this point in the summer, all the grasses looked like dried brush, and wheatgrass was everywhere anyway. I took the arrowhead out of my pocket and stared at it. I had been given a directive, and I intended to keep it.

As I reached a location that seemed approximate, I knelt on the ground. *Should I say a few words?* Summoning any Presbyterian teachings I absorbed as a child, I melded them with what I imagined to be Kima's beliefs.

"Creator God," I said, looking up into the sky. "I'm returning this arrowhead to its rightful home. To the ancestors who left it here." Not particularly eloquent, but it's all that came to mind.

I lowered my gaze and placed the quartz artifact back among the pebbled landscape, gently, as if releasing a bird with a healed wing. As my fingertips touched the ground, a powerful feeling of connectedness welled up inside me. My hand felt rooted through the soil, into the very bedrock below. Tendrils of awareness spread from my fingers across the plain. I was part of the hills, the sky overhead, the faint trace of the setting half-melon moon on the horizon. We were all linked in a delicate, neuron-like web. I could feel rather than hear the calls of ancient creatures that had once roamed across the landscape. These vibrations were overlain by ones of extinction and despair. The ghosts of native people who died here seemed to hover in the shadows and the crevasses.

I rose from the ground and the air stilled. The sensation melted away like ice in the desert, and I was left once more, staring into the distance. My skin shivered in the sun. It felt like a sacred moment.

———————

I arrived at my fossil plant site, which shined in the undulating sunlight. The multicolored layers of siltstone and shale seemed to shift in my view. Pale pink patches formed from long-ago burned lignite juxtaposed with the gray and tan strata. I pulled out my rock hammer and began to dislodge more rocks from the cliff. One by one they fell to the earth, man-made erosion allowing gravity to do its work. I knelt on the ground and began splitting a chunk of siltstone along a bedding plane, revealing carbon films of leaves. Here was evidence of the past lives of the ancient organisms, the plants that had fed the herbivores, which had in turn nourished the carnivores. With the ream of work already published on the Cretaceous flora, would these discoveries amount to anything important? It was true that perhaps I could collaborate with others. But I yearned to discover something of value, and now I was unsure I would find it here.

My stomach gurgled and I leaned over my backpack, reaching inside for my peanut butter sandwich. A chuffing sound caused me to raise my head. My eyes widened at the sight in front of me. My body froze in fear.

Not ten feet away stood an enormous bison. Its furry head bobbled up and down. Two sharp horns glistened in the light. A cloven hoof stamped aggressively on the ground. I sucked in my breath as I slowly straightened. Taking two steps backward, I flattened myself against the cliff. Nothing but the backpack in my shaking hand stood between us. My heart ricocheted around my chest. Reading my *Western Wildlife* book had in no way prepared me for this moment. *Bison bison*, I thought stupidly, as if the taxonomy would help me. What had Rob said? Stay away from them? Well, good luck there.

The bison gazed at me with its cowlike eyes. I stared back, not daring to breathe or make a sound. It tilted its bearded head as if to study me and flicked its long, gray tongue. Then it made a sound between a growl and a low roar, turned aside, and took a few steps away. I watched its tail swoosh from side to side like a pendulum, hoping the animal would keep going. But it stopped, turned its mighty cranium back around, and considered me as if wanting me to follow.

I kept still, my limbs frozen. A few minutes passed, which seemed like hours, both of us at a standstill. Its intense eyes held my gaze. We were at an impasse, it seemed, so I slowly bent my shaking knees and wrapped my hand around the handle of my rock hammer. I began to inch along toward the animal, my back still plastered against the cliff. The bison turned its head and continued to amble away. Then again it stopped, looking back almost as if to make sure I was in pursuit. It moaned again and flicked its tail. I began to wonder if the animal was domesticated. It seemed almost tame.

The bison reached the end of the hillock and, with a loud grunt, disappeared around the corner. I gulped down my fear and peeked my head around to gauge its distance. The animal waited until I was in view, then kept walking along the backside of the hill. I rounded the edge and scooched along, my shoulder still pressed against the cliff. After treading a few more minutes, the creature gave me one last look, issued a final snort, and seemingly satisfied, loped away across the plain with its strange hump-backed gait.

My heart rate began to decrescendo, like a jet engine landing on a runway. I breathed in and out to refill my lungs, almost hyperventilating, and slid down to the ground, dropping my hammer next to me. Slowly, my breath returned to normal as I watched the rump of the bison in the far distance. Eventually, it disappeared from view, blending into the brown expanse of earth and the mirage of endless sky.

I sat motionless against the hillslope until my hunger returned. My hand rooted around for the sandwich inside my pack and I unwrapped it, biting distractedly into the peanut butter wedge. As I chewed, I pondered. The bison had certainly snuck up on me. I hadn't heard it approach. Where had it come from? Did it live out here, all alone in the badlands?

Finished with my sandwich, I rose and brushed the dirt off my pants. I surveyed my new surroundings, having never ventured this far from my site. The topography along the backside of the hillock sloped downward, which caused lower layers of rock to become exposed. The paleosol horizon containing the plant fossils now reached inaccessibly above my head. I turned toward the newly exposed lower strata. Several terra-cotta-colored rock lenses looked out of place within the olive-gray beds. They were stacked vertically, separated from each other by several feet. Upon close inspection, I realized they were composed of coarse sandstone and not silt and clay like everything else.

Could these have been small stream channels cutting through the otherwise swampy environment?

I used my hammer to do a little investigating. As I dug into the hillside, a large chunk of olive-gray clay fell away between two sandstone lenses. To my surprise, the sandstones were not lenses but were connected as part of the same elongated vertical column. About a foot and a half wide, the column extended down, bisecting the horizontal beds and cutting across the layers. More investigation revealed that the column began at the paleosol and stretched at least five feet in length. I knew it must be younger than the surrounding rocks according to the law of cross-cutting relationships. Now its shape was all wrong to be an ancient stream channel. But what was it? Something compelling, I was sure of that. My heart rate once again picked up as I wondered at the possibilities.

I continued digging at this new location, the cliff towering above me. More sandstone stringers came into view. They looked like parallel infilled tunnels with vaguely corkscrew shapes. I took a few careful strikes into the surrounding claystone at the sandstone edges. The encasing rock chipped away, exposing the harder strands. More resistant to weathering than the surrounding rock, they jutted out slightly in relief once I exposed them.

Intrigued, I went to work at the base, hammering, my knees pressed into the ground. I worked my way upward, stretching along the cliff to fully expose one of the sandstone stringers. It was round in three dimensions. Two short side shoots poked out horizontally, also infilled with sandstone. As I uncovered one of the horizontal side tunnels it occurred to me.

I had discovered a petrified animal burrow.

Rob stared at me, incredulous, from across the fire. He leaned forward from his rock perch, elbows on his knees. "What?" he said. "Let me get this straight—you saw a bison? Up close?"

The chemical stench from the briquettes stung my eyes, but I reminded myself of its mosquito-repelling properties. I blinked as I nodded. "Yep. It was as close to me as you are now."

"You're joking. What did you do when you saw it?" he asked.

"I stood still, up against the hillside. Until it started to walk away."

Theo moved into the fire circle and joined in the conversation. "You saw a bison?" he asked, settling down on another rock. "How big was it?"

"Hmm . . . bigger than a cow, I guess," I said, crinkling my brow in concentration. The entire episode seemed almost dreamlike as if I'd imagined it.

"And it was alone?"

"Yep. Just the one."

Rob took over the questioning. "Did it look healthy? Was it well fed?"

I shook my head. "I don't know. How can you tell if a bison is healthy? It didn't exactly give me a medical report."

"Did it have a thick coat?"

I thought for a moment and shrugged. "I guess so."

"Was it a male or a female?"

I squinted at Rob. "Just how would I know that?"

"The males are bigger. And the females have horns that point inward."

"Well, there was only one, so I couldn't compare. And I didn't know that about the horns."

"Did you notice *anything* about it?" he asked.

I thought for a moment. "It didn't seem to want to hurt me," I said.

I turned my head to study the western horizon, the sky splattered with the carmine stripes of sunset, and recalled my close encounter with the bison. The one thing that stood out in my mind was an image of its soulful nut-brown eyes.

———

"What do you think?" I asked Frank, handing him a chunk of sandstone. I had extracted a piece from the new location and brought it home in my knapsack.

He turned it over in his hands, examining the specimen. "Let me get this straight. A buffalo led you to this?" he asked.

"Technically, a bison. The term 'buffalo' was incorrectly used by early French explorers."

"Okay, and this *bison* wanted you to follow it?" he asked in a doubtful tone. He raised his eyebrows at me.

"Maybe," I said, anxious to move on from the bison. "What do you think about the rock?"

He ignored my question. "You encountering a bison is exactly why I don't like you exploring on your own."

"Yes, you've covered that."

He breathed out a sigh through his nostrils. "I guess I'll stop beating that dead horse." His attention turned back to the sample. "So this rock is part of a vertical pipe, cutting across the bedding? And the top is at the paleosol?" he asked.

"Yep."

He nodded. "I think you're right. It's probably a tunnel of some sort."

"Do you think it could be an animal burrow?"

"Maybe. It's too big to be a crawfish tunnel or a scorpion nest. How many are there?"

"As many as ten. I have to spend more time uncovering them. At first I thought they were stream channel lenses because only parts are exposed," I answered.

"And they're composed of this sandstone?"

"Yes, the lithology is coarser than the surrounding layers. The tunnels are all similar—same color, same texture. Like they were infilled during a single flood event."

Frank turned the rock over and looked at it closely with his hand lens, his head bent in concentration. "That makes sense."

"If they're burrows, maybe I'll find vegetation inside if the critter lined its home with leaves to make a nest. Or if I'm really lucky, I might find a skeleton inside one."

I grabbed the chunk of sandstone back from him and held it up in front of us with both hands. I paused and took a deep breath. "What type of creature, sixty-five million years ago, might have dug this burrow?"

Frank shrugged. "Who knows? Mammal fossils the size of badgers have been discovered from the Cretaceous. Or it could have been a reptile. Or even a small dinosaur. Do you think these burrows are more interesting scientifically than your plant fossils?"

I replied, "Yes, I think these have more potential for a big discovery. Whether the site pans out is another matter. There might be nothing inside any of them."

"Great. So you've left me for the whole summer to pound on sandstone stringers." Frank sent me a hard look. "And why, exactly, aren't you showing this to Dr. Small?"

I paused, biting my lip. "I'm not quite sure why. I have a feeling that something's being hidden from me. The men seem eager for me to leave every morning, and they cover the dinosaur bones with tarps when they see me coming back. If they're not going to share their findings with me, then I'm not going to show this to them."

"They probably don't want to share intellectual property with you. Then they'd have to put your name on their publications."

I paused and stared back at Frank.

Could that be the reason I was being iced out?

"I never thought of that," I said.

"If Theo publishes and includes the team, whose name would go first on the publication?"

"It's usually alphabetical. So mine would go first. Ballantine," I said.

"Exactly. And he wouldn't want that, would he? That's probably why he's keeping the bones a secret from you."

My eyebrows arched as I considered the possibility, and frustration built in my chest at the thought of being excluded from future publications.

"Well, two can play at that game," I said.

Could my burrows have housed a mammal of some sort? Or were they the dwelling places of reptiles or amphibians? With so many burrows, could the animals have lived in a colony?

I ruminated on these questions over breakfast that Sunday. Then I remembered where I had seen a colony of burrows. Grabbing my *Western Wildlife* book, I paged past the photo of a bison, giving an involuntary shiver, and stopped at the section on prairie dogs. I began to read.

"Frank, listen to this. The black-tailed prairie dog, *Cynomys ludovicianus*, is not related to dogs but is a rodent. A type of ground squirrel. The prairie dog is herbivorous and eats mostly seeds, roots, and grasses. They especially like blue grama and buffalo grass."

"Uh-huh," he said, smothering a piece of toast with jelly.

"They live in towns, like we saw in the badlands, and each town can house up to twenty-five family groups, which are called coteries."

"Are you thinking your tunnels are from prairie dogs?"

"No. It says here that prairie dog fossils are rare, but they've only been found back to the Plio-Pleistocene, about two or three million years ago. So my burrows weren't dug by prairie dogs in the Cretaceous. But if they have similar features, that might suggest that mine were dug by mammals."

"How long are prairie dog burrows?" he asked, taking a bite of toast.

"They're extensive—over thirty feet long, and vertically they can extend ten feet below the ground. And they have multiple entrances."

"Hmm, so they're longer horizontally than vertically?"

"Right. So not the same as the fossil burrows that I've found, which are longer vertically. Still, both have chambers. Prairie dog burrows have different chambers that serve different functions. There are chambers for sleeping, chambers to avoid predators, and nursery chambers for the young. The nursery chambers are the deepest and are lined with grass. They even have a separate chamber for pooping. When it fills up, they dig a new one."

"Interesting. Although I think it's too early to discount reptiles or amphibians digging your tunnels."

I flipped a page in the book. "Or they could have been mammal dens, but taken over by another animal. Black-footed ferrets eat prairie dogs and move into their burrows. Snakes and owls have been known to nest in them too."

"Lots of possibilities. Maybe you should concentrate on the side chambers. If you're hoping to find a skeleton, that's probably where you'll find one."

"Yeah, that's what I was thinking," I said.

Now I had a plan.

CHAPTER 24

The mission to uncover the burrows spurred me on through the heat and the muscle aches. I wiped the sweat away from my forehead and groaned as I rose off the ground. The long North Dakota summer days ticked along, the sun repeatedly crossing the meridian. By serendipity, the sky remained cloudless most days. I had exhumed, scraped, excavated, measured, and documented several of the burrows. The burrows were filled with sandstone and nothing else, at least so far. I concentrated on the inside of the horizontal resting chambers. However, upon scraping through the infilling sandstone, no bones appeared. It was as if the animals had all scampered away before a flood drowned their homes. Maybe some escaped. But I did not think all the critters could have been that lucky.

And I hoped to have some luck myself.

The day waning, I began to hike back across the prairie to camp. Plant fossils filled my knapsack, a bit of subterfuge in case anyone asked about my progress. As the field crew grew larger in my vision, an animated discussion seemed ongoing. The three men stood around the dinosaur site. Theo pointed at the bones, his arms waving as he exclaimed about something on the ground. As I drew closer, the men spied me, halting their conversation. By the time I arrived, the tarps had been pulled over the bones.

I walked to my tent and dropped my knapsack. My shoulders sagged and my knees complained. My face was a pool of grit.

Ignoring the men, I made my way to one of the trucks and lowered the tailgate. Pouring a little water into our wash basin, I scrubbed my hands with a bar of Ivory soap and splashed water on my face. Time to start my second shift.

The flame of the camp stove ignited with a whiff of propane. Tonight's meal would be sloppy joes made with canned corn beef. I opened the can and slid the block of meat into a frying pan. The beef sizzled, browning on the edges. I chopped the block into pieces with a metal spatula. Salt and pepper. I added canned tomato sauce. After a long day of hammering, the aroma made my stomach growl.

"Dinner's ready!" I called.

I ladled the sloppy joe mixture onto slices of white bread as the men brought over their mess kits. A mess indeed, at least tonight.

Carrying my dinner over to the firepit, I lowered onto my usual rock. Rob settled down next to me, balancing his plate on his knees.

"See any bison today?" he asked.

"Nope, not today," I replied.

"How'd your digging go?" he asked.

"Fine." I shrugged. "I found a few more leaves."

He took a bite of his sloppy joe and wiped his mouth with his sleeve. "Groovy. Have at it. We're able to handle the bones here."

"Anything worthwhile here today?" I asked.

"Not really. Same stuff. Most are broken up. Theo's not sure they'll be worth jacketing and transporting."

A broken record, that.

I wondered how long one could play a broken record before the cracks splintered into sharp shards of distrust.

After two weeks of hard labor, more burrows and chambers stood out in relief against the darker rocks of the hillside. I exposed them, measured the lengths of each segment, and documented the cork-screw twists and the angles of the turns. My field notebook was filled with calculations and sketches. Something had dug these chambers, with claws or paws, feet or teeth. The critter had been fairly small. Dinosaur or lizard? Monotreme or marsupial? No rodents or rabbits had yet evolved by Cretaceous time. The burrows seemed to taunt me with these unanswered questions. Each time I unearthed a resting chamber at the tunnel base, I carefully scraped through the sandstone filling hoping to find a skeleton. Where were the bones of these creatures? Or fossil vegetation left from nests? So far, nothing. Until.

Late morning, the sun beat down on my back as I tried to shelter under a slight overhang. My face studied the outcrop. A tiny sharp edge of something stuck out of a side chamber. Not the resting chamber at the bottom of the burrow but a short diversion halfway down. I reached for my rock hammer and scratched next to the sliver with the pick end. Blowing away the grains, a white protrusion came into view. I set down my hammer and reached into my backpack for a finer pick. With tiny movements, I excised the fragment. It fell out into my hand. I stared down at it. It was about a centimeter in length and irregular in shape. Reaching for my hand lens on the string around my neck, I magnified the surface. Pits and bumps revealed themselves under magnification.

My pulse quickened. It was not my expertise, but I recognized the texture of an eggshell when I saw it. A fossil eggshell fragment. From a sixty-five-million-year-old egg.

"Woo-hoo! Finally!" I called out to no one.

But I still had a lot to learn. Did the animal that lived in this burrow lay eggs? Or scavenge and eat them?

The rest of the afternoon I meticulously chipped at the rock, removing sand grains with careful swipes of my pick and brush. The exhumed edges of a dozen eggshell fragments peeked from the rock. I carefully broke off the sandstone block containing them. Wrapping the chunk in an entire roll of paleo paper, I slipped the specimen into a canvas sample bag.

My hands shook as I zipped the package with utmost care into my knapsack, like a priest handling a holy relic.

In the western sky, a cumulonimbus cloud lifted its mass of water droplets, ice crystals, and water vapor, smacking an anvil-shaped head against the stratosphere. Its blackened base threatened an oncoming storm, a signal for me to hike back.

As I once again trekked across the prairie, I wondered, *Did the bison bring me to this new discovery?*

I shook off the superstitious thought. I was a scientist. Period. None of that fanciful thinking for me.

In sight of the camp, I watched Theo covering a corner of the dinosaur excavation. He, too, looked worriedly at the developing cloud in the distance. Hans and Rob picked up the shovels and trowels and placed them on top of the tarp to weigh it down.

"How did your day go?" I asked as I approached. "Any progress?"

Rob looked up. "Not really. Some leg bones are there, and a few disarticulated vertebrae."

Hans glanced at Rob with a knowing expression on his face. Rob returned a nervous smile. Observing the smirk on Hans's face caused something inside me to snap, like the loosening of a last guitar string. I furrowed my brow and glared at them. Any tiny vestige of trust I had in these men evaporated like virga into the ether.

"How about you, Henrietta? Find anything interesting today?"

"Nope," I replied. "Not a thing."

Night descended and the west wind howled across the plain, turning our camp into a sea of flapping canvas. The warmed air, lifting throughout the day, built an inferno of low pressure. We battened down our supplies and crawled into our tents. Gusts whined around the excavation site, carrying pebbly grit, slamming into the trucks, and lifting tarps. Shovels toppled and clanged, the pitches ringing above the sighs and thrums. I hunkered in my sleeping bag and stared as the sides of my pup tent inflated and shimmied. My knapsack and boots rested in the corner. My precious sandstone containing the eggshells nestled inside my duffel bag, protected by my dirty clothes.

One thought came to my mind, however. The storm would provide a perfect cover for me to investigate the dinosaur site.

I rolled over and extracted my legs out of the cottony embrace of my sleeping bag. The top of my tent whacked at my head as I sat up. I leaned over toward a corner and felt for my flashlight. Finding the metal cylinder, I grasped it and clicked it on. With a low battery, the flashlight emitted only a faint elliptical bull's-eye. Good enough. I grabbed my boots and strapped my feet inside them. Not caring if I looked ridiculous in my pajamas and boots, I unzipped my tent and crawled out into the night.

The sky held the blackish-purple hue of kiln-darkened amethyst. Cloud-to-cloud lightning flitted like angry fairies, illuminating the cumulonimbus overhead. I headed toward the dinosaur site, keeping the flashlight beam low to the ground. My long hair whipped around my face, unbraided and untamed, and my eyes watered in the wind. The flashlight beam wobbled as I walked on the uneven ground. My limbs shivered, not from the cold but from the wind's moaning. I raked the light beam back and forth at my feet. Sand blew across the ground, hitting my pajama pants.

A whipping sound came from the adjacent hill, in the direction of the dig site. I swung the flashlight in that direction and walked forward with the beam. As I approached, I could see one of the tarps was loose, flapping in the gale. I looked back at the camp, but nothing moved. Pushing ahead, I walked along the edge of the dig site, not wanting to plunge into a hole. Part of the excavation surface was exposed as the top corner of a loose tarp whipped with punishing fury. I stepped forward and grabbed for it, but it evaded my reach. Instead, it lashed across my face, a metal grommet catching my chin. I snapped back, my hand to my face. Blood trickled from a gash on my chin. I pressed my sleeve against the cut to stop the bleeding. As I did, my flashlight washed over the excavation surface.

The pit was several feet deeper than when I had last been allowed to see it. The men had been busy digging and trenching. What had I just seen on the lower exposed surface? I knelt and crawled under the flapping tarp, then lowered myself into the hole. Holding the flashlight in one hand, I ran the beam over the ground. A gasp filled my lungs.

Wide eye sockets in a gigantic skull jeered at me from under the waving shroud. Sinister razor-sharp teeth protruded from a massive jawbone. The unmistakable outlines of the thick bones appeared in the glow beneath my feet. This was no duck-billed dinosaur. Nor was it a ceratopsian.

This site contained a theropod, a bipedal meat-eater, and an enormous one at that. There was not a doubt in my mind.

I was kneeling at the grave of a *Tyrannosaurus rex*.

CHAPTER 25

"Everybody all right after last night's blow?" Theo asked as he lumbered out of his tent.

Evidence of the windstorm littered the camp. The rain had been brief, but the wind compensated, howling throughout most of the night. Silt shrouded the damp canvases and dulled the metal of the trucks. Our water jugs, cooler, and canned goods were covered in dirt. Tent poles tilted leeward. Last night, I had managed to batten down the flapping tarp at the dig site, covering any evidence of my stealthy excursion.

The propane stove, newly wiped down and lit, hissed on a tailgate. Simmering on top of it, the morning coffee yielded a tantalizing scent, pulling the men like a magnetic force. My anger simmered as well, the results of my evening's sleuthing burning in my chest. As far as I knew, no *T. rex* skeletons had been discovered since Barnum Brown's discoveries in the early twentieth century. This was a major find, and the men were excluding me from it.

My brain burned with anger. This was like a mirror to my time in graduate school, where lab equipment became unavailable and invitations to seminars mysteriously missed my mailbox. Where academic discussions conveniently cropped up in the coffee room during my teaching hours. Where my work was scrutinized to a degree unknown to my fellow male students. Well, I'd had enough.

Rob walked up to me and stared. "What happened to your chin?"

My hand flew up to my face. "Oh, just a little cut. A mishap with my hammer. It's fine."

"I didn't notice it last night, or I would've offered you a Band-Aid. Do you want one?"

"Sure," I said, wishing I had looked in the truck's side mirror.

He opened the cab door and reached in for the first-aid kit. "Here," he said, walking back to me and popping it open. "Let me put some Bactine on it." He squirted the liquid antiseptic on a cotton ball and dabbed it on my face.

"Ouch, that stings."

"Yeah, I know. Hold still." He tore the wrapper off a Band-Aid and stuck it along the edge of my jaw.

Theo walked over with his metal cup and gripped the coffee pot handle like it was a savior. He poured the liquid and took a giant slurp. "We're gonna leave for town by early afternoon today, so be sure you're back by then. If you're not here, I'll call you on the walkie-talkie when we start packing up."

I tried to maintain a neutral tone even as I was raging inside. "All right. I'll toss my tent and duffel in the truck before I hike out," I said.

Reaching for the can opener, I removed the lids from our last three cans of potted meat and slammed the cans down. I grabbed the ends of our loaves of Wonder Bread and undid the twist ties. By Friday, the white bread was still weirdly fresh yet especially tasteless, even if it did "build strong bodies twelve ways."

"Breakfast is ready," I said, grim-faced. "End of the groceries for the week. Make it last."

Everybody groaned.

I puffed out a deep breath and took in the view of the vertical sandstone-filled tunnels, now standing out in etched relief after my intense digging to expose them. Were these lairs for extinct egg-stealing mammals? Or hideaways for egg-laying dinosaurs?

I grabbed my hammer and approached the final burrow. The eggshells had been found in a side chamber. Perhaps this burrow would be the lucky one. Could there be an unseen offshoot, extending into the hill? I wedged my hammer around the edges of the burrow, trying to expose the backside.

Then an idea roared to the front of my brain. I had measured, diagrammed, and documented this burrow—at least the portions that I could reach. Would it be a terrible crime to remove it, exposing any chambers that extended behind it, into the outcrop? Was there some unwritten rule to protect it? And who was following rules now, anyway? Certainly not the men running this excursion. My hike across the plain had done nothing to defuse my anger at them. Frustration built up in me, like a steam engine ready to pop.

I stepped back and analyzed the exposed burrows. Lots of burrows. Fossil eggs found in only this one.

No one was here to see me. After all, the men had banished me from the dinosaur site as if I were a pesky mosquito. Well, I was tired of being shoved aside and lied to.

I took my hammer and slammed it forcefully into the terra-cotta sandstone. The burrow fell away in chunks, landing at my feet.

I hollered with all my lungs' strength. "A *T. rex*! They found a *T. rex*! And not one word to me about it. 'Nothing but broken bones,' they said."

Whack!

"'Not worth excavating,' they said!" The blood raced in my veins. *Chop! Hack!*

Any overflying birds would have gazed down and thought a crazy woman had been let loose.

"'Throw the tarps over it. Here she comes. Cover it up.'" I shouted toward the sky. "'Let's not share our discovery! Let's not share authorship! We don't want her on our publications!'"

My imagination flailed on and on, along with my flogging hammer.

Sweat bathed my brow and soaked my shirt. I rubbed my hand across my cheeks. Finally, I stopped, my lungs gasping, my arms roaring. Leaning over, I dropped my hammer and rested my hands on my knees. Segments and splinters of sandstone littered the base of the cliff like broken roof shingles. I gave a small, slightly hysterical laugh. I had done a first-class job of wreckage. As I raised my eyes to the cliff, I saw that the lowermost five vertical feet of burrow had been destroyed.

So much for that burrow.

But my heart gave a small leap of joy. For in its place, once hidden, an elliptical cross-section of sandstone had been revealed. The distinctive shape marked the presence of another side chamber, extending horizontally into the hill. I held my breath. Would it contain anything valuable?

This time, my digging was drill-like, boring into the hill, an encircling excavation to isolate the chamber of sandstone. As the surrounding rock gave way, I pulled the excess debris toward me and dumped it on the ground. I began to feel like a kindred spirit with the animal that had dug this chamber in the first place. The terra-cotta sandstone extended for about two feet into the hill. After an hour of excavation, it was almost free. I pulled on it with all my strength, my feet against the cliff, my arms and back straining. It loosened. I slid a thick chisel around to the far end and rapped on it with my hammer. A few well-placed strikes and the final cemented bond broke. I yanked on it again, and slowly, slowly, the sandstone chamber scraped out from the enclosing rock.

I held it in my hands like manna. The moment of truth. Setting the stone on the ground, I held a small wedge against it and gave it a tap with my hammer. A slice of terra-cotta slivered off the top. Nothing uncovered. I moved the wedge a quarter inch and gave it another tap. More sandstone cleaved off.

Then I saw a shine of ecru. I held the rock up to my eye and lifted my hand lens from around my neck. Staring through the magnifier, a glimmer of hope passed through me.

The sun had reached its southerly point, indicating noon, but my stomach fluttered in anticipation rather than hunger, as if I had swallowed a kaleidoscope of butterflies. Unzipping a pocket, I grabbed my smallest dental pick. With meticulous whittling, my spirits lifted higher. Something was buried here, I felt sure of it. Exposed by my careful swipes, thin, fragile bones began to peek through the sediment grains. My heart raced faster. Could that be part of a tiny vertebra? Or perhaps the edge of a cranium? The animal was small, this I knew. But it was there, trapped in an instant, caught in a flood, and wondrously preserved throughout geological time.

The men had found a *T. rex*. But I had uncovered something too. My precious discovery.

As much as I wanted to continue, I knew this kind of preparation had to be completed delicately in the lab. I needed to get the eggshells and bones to Mary. She was the only one I trusted. I pulled a new roll of paleo paper from my knapsack and wound it around and around the bone-encasing rock, cushioning it as best as I could. I slid it into a large canvas sample bag and nestled it inside my knapsack, filling its interior.

It was time for me to hike back. Probably past time, and the weight of the sandstone block would slow me down. Theo would be angry if I were late. But I needed to finish my measurements. This last burrow now took on added importance, being the one containing my discovery. I needed to measure its length to the top entrance, which was above my head. The uppermost part of the burrow, which I had not destroyed, began at a level I could not reach from the ground. I stared upward. *Could I climb up there?*

A sinuous, eroded gully snaked up one side of the hill. My boot would just fit inside the width of the cleft. Perhaps I could climb above the top of the tunnel and measure from overhead? I stuck a tape measure into my back pocket, marched to the base of the eroded channel, and began to climb. Gravel rained down under my sliding feet as I placed one boot in front of the other in the crack. I took my time, bending over, jabbing my rock hammer's pick into the ground in front of me to stabilize the climb. *Careful, careful.* My breath raced as I reached a point above the burrow's entrance. I lowered myself to a kneel, leaned over, and began to lower the end of the tape measure. Realizing I did not have the best angle, I reached my arm farther out, trying to hold the ruler vertically.

Instantaneously, I felt the slide, as if the world was tilting in front of me. Talus loosened under my knees. Leaning with my arm outstretched, I had no time to react or utter a cry. I dropped the tape measure. My rock hammer skidded off the ledge and I tumbled after it, falling along the front of the cliff.

Pulled by the mass of the earth, I banged onto the ground below.

Fog settled in my brain. Lying prostrate, I emitted a low moan from the back of my throat, like a damaged wildebeest. My abdomen was a basket of fire. I realized one of my arms was trapped beneath me. Agony shot through my limbs. I tried to press up with my unrestrained arm, but pain ricocheted from my shoulder to my wrist. My head slumped back down and my cheek pressed back into the dirt. Darkness descended. My mind fell down a vault and began to dream.

Rising from the ground like a giant eagle, my arms extended without pain. I sailed over a continent, across a vast sea, to Africa. Rhinos, hippos, and elephants meandered below me, oblivious to my tropospheric snooping. I soared over the parched ground of Olduvai Gorge, looped around an acacia tree, and skimmed over the sisal, toward the Leakey camp. Tents flapped and a dalmatian barked. A monkey hooted at me from the lean-to banda.

Squawk!

The scent of gooey plaster encasing fossil fish lifted to my nose. The Leakey quarry passed beneath me, the familiar multicolored strata gleaming along the stair-stepped escarpment. Across I flew to a familiar excavated dig site, once the crypt of a fossil woman. Heat lightning crackled. Static seemed to fill the void.

Screech! "Henrietta, are you there?"

A shadow fell across me, a humanlike shape. Was that a hand pressing on my shoulder? Words reverberated through my being, wispy, as if carried on the wind.

"Rest now, sister."

Squawk! "Henrietta, come in. Do you need help?"

In the dim recesses of my brain, did I hear a question? My lips could not begin to form an answer.

To my ears, the wind increased, whooshing like the gust front preceding the wall cloud of a tornadic storm. The noise rose, buzzing like static.

Screech!

And then the blackness won.

Raised voices cut across my subconscious. I was dimly aware of the scuttling of boots. An engine growled and brakes squealed. I jarred awake as I was loaded like a mummy into the back seat, encased in a woolen blanket smeared in blood. The truck shot across the badlands, jamming into the arroyos, crushing between the buttes. The back of the passenger seat provided my only view, rising and falling as we plunged onward. Tears watered my cheeks. The spasming of my gut made me grit my teeth as moans escaped from my lips.

"Hang on, Henrietta!" I heard Rob call to me.

Each bounce speared me with agony. My body rose and slammed down onto the seat. My useless arms were trapped in the blanket like vestigial appendages. Blood slickened my hands.

With the relief of a thousand angels, we found the smooth macadam of the highway and raced toward civilization.

CHAPTER 26

I awoke, groggy, in a gray room with a lingering aroma of stale coffee and antiseptic. Frank sat on a chair next to my bed, his face a mask of worry. Bags underscored his half-closed eyes like dark saucers. I groaned and tried to sit up.

"What happened?" I whispered, my voice sounding oddly croaky.

Relief crept into his eyes. "My God, Henrietta, you scared me half to death," he said.

"I found something, Frank," I said, my throat a parched desert.

"Just lie back and rest."

"Something important. There's a *T. rex*."

"What?" He leaned toward me.

"A *T. rex*," I whispered.

"You found a *T. rex*?" he asked.

"No, not me." I winced in pain. "I found something else."

He wiped his hand across his face. "You must have had a bad dream. You're in the hospital, honey."

I groaned again and reached for my head. A herd of wild stallions pounded across my cerebrum.

"How do you feel?" he asked.

"Fuzzy," I said, cotton-mouthed.

"You fell. In the field. Do you remember?"

I tried to nod, which was a bad idea. "My head hurts. Can I have some water?"

"Sure." He reached over and grabbed a cup with a straw. Holding my head up in one hand, he let me take a slow sip.

"Ah, thank you. What day is it?"

"It's Saturday. You fell yesterday. You landed on your rock hammer."

A vision of the back seat of a truck came into my mind. "I remember there was blood."

"That's an understatement. You broke your arm. And you've had emergency surgery."

"Surgery for what?"

"You're still coming out of the anesthesia. The doctor should be in soon." He patted my hand as if I were a child, which worried me as much as anything.

I dozed in and out, assaulted by fragmented memories of eggshells and bones, rhinos and monkeys, overlain by the roar of the wind. I was dimly aware when the doctor came through the door, a lab-coated apparition to my half-awake subconscious.

Frank rose from his chair and met him. In an undertone, the two men consulted as if I were an inanimate object taking up space in the room. I could barely make out their words.

"Your wife's lucky . . . gotten here when she did. She's . . . blood. She'll make a full recovery but . . . take time."

I could see relief creep into Frank's eyes.

The doctor continued, "We repaired several tears in her abdomen." He cleared his throat and lowered his voice even further. "Unfortunately, after this . . . a significant amount of abdominal scar tissue. Which means . . . chance of her being able to carry a child . . . low to nil."

His words penetrated through my fog, searing into my psyche like an incandescent pyroclastic cloud.

Frank turned his face toward me, his eyes bloodshot, his shoulders slumped. Trying to speak, his words seemed to stick in his throat as if he were swallowing a mountain of misery.

"But she'll be okay, though, right?" he asked.

"Yes, indeed." The doctor walked over and leaned down in front of my face. "How do you feel, Mrs. Bailey?" he asked loudly, in a slow cadence, as if I were a deaf kindergartener.

"Groggy," I whispered, my eyes slit against the light.

He patted the cast on my arm. "Just get some rest. Everything will be all right. The nurses will take good care of you."

I watched him walk out the door, leaving his condescension hanging behind him like a fine mist.

How could he know I would be all right?

And what did it mean that along the tattered edges of my conscious mind, I felt a mixture of both grief and relief?

The alabaster ceiling in my hospital room hung over my head like a dimpled shroud. I was tired of counting the pits in the tiles. A monitor beeped and an alarm sounded down the hall, making my head throb. The stench of bleach mingled with that of leftover scrambled eggs on my breakfast tray. Under my gown, a wide smile-shaped incision crossed my abdomen. An oxymoron of a wound, the smile flared red and inflamed like an angry crescent moon. Black stitches crisscrossed my belly.

After four days, Frank had gone back to work and I was alone, left with a grumpy lump of a nurse who occasionally slipped in to adjust my monitor as if it were an imposition instead of her job.

The phone on the bedside table rang, a shrill clanging in my ear. I groaned as I reached over and grabbed the receiver.

"Hello?" I croaked.

"Henrietta, this is your mother. Thank heavens you picked up."

"Oh, hello, Mother. How are you?"

"How am I?" she asked, her voice indignant. "How are you? Frank called us last night and told us about your accident. Why he didn't call us right away is beyond me."

I sighed inwardly. "He'd been here with me. In the hospital. He finally went home so he could call you long distance. And get some sleep."

"He said you'd fallen?"

"Yes, I fell on my rock hammer. I had to have abdominal surgery. But I'm all right. I'll be fine in a month or so."

"I told your dad that we need to make flight reservations and come out there. But he said to talk to you first."

My nerves prickled at that statement. Entertaining my parents, especially my mother, would drain any energy I possessed out of my body. "Oh, you don't have to come here. There's nothing you could do except watch me sleep. And I still plan to come home in September. I'll be fine by then," I said, having no idea if that were true.

"Well, if you're sure. We don't want to be in the way."

Relief coursed through me. "I'll be fine. Really."

"I told you and your dad that all that hammering and climbing wasn't safe for a young woman. But did the two of you listen? Oh, no. Not one bit."

"Nope, sorry, Mother. Not one bit."

We said our goodbyes, and I settled the receiver back on the cradle. Outside my window, a few spidery cirrus clouds wafted across the troposphere, marring an otherwise clear, robin-egg sky. It would be a perfect field day.

But not for me, I pouted.

I could not believe I had fallen. Of all the stupid stunts. Now I was bashed, bruised, and sewn together like a ridiculous Raggedy Ann doll. I guess I should be thankful I had not sustained bigger injuries, but instead, I was stuck here, griping to myself about the loss of the remaining field season. And fending off my mother.

Deep inside, though, I knew this was a distraction from facing the real issue, the bigger one. The one between Frank and me. I would probably never have children. We had not talked about it since the doctor's pronouncement. How did I feel about this new truth, underneath all the bruises and bandages? I had never given much thought to having a child. I always focused on the next step to becoming a paleontologist. College. Graduate school. But I had met Frank, and he assumed we would have a family. I had put him off, with the standard "someday" answer. Weren't women's roles changing? Did all women have to want to become mothers? Betty Friedan said we should be equal partners with men and founded a movement to make it happen.

But my ruminations did not answer my internal question. The one I needed to solve at my core.

Had I ever wanted to become a mother?

And now, it seemed the question had been answered for me. I felt tears pool behind my eyes.

A tentative knock sounded on the half-closed door. Mary Tremaine peeked in, clutching an arrangement of daisies.

I wiped my tears with the back of my hand.

"Oh, Mary. Come in!"

"I don't want to intrude," Mary said, walking toward me with a soft smile. "How are you feeling?" She set the daisies down on the side table.

"You aren't intruding. I could use the company," I said, sniffling. "Thank you for the flowers. They're lovely. I'm feeling cranky and sore, to be honest."

Mary chuckled. "Well, I know you're always honest." She pulled up a chair and sat by my bed. "I heard about your fall. I'm so sorry. Wally is too. He told me to tell you that he hopes you recover soon."

"Yes, I fell from a cliff. I was up high and leaning over and lost my balance. I should have known better. I was out of sight of the rest of the crew. It's a miracle they found me as fast as they did."

"Hans told Wally that they heard you on the walkie-talkie. So they knew you were in trouble."

I stared at her. "What?"

"The walkie-talkie. He said you carried one in case you needed help. You called on it after you fell."

I took a moment and searched my murky memory. "I didn't call on the walkie-talkie. It was attached to my knapsack. I didn't fall anywhere near it."

She shrugged. "That's what he said. Maybe you crawled to it? After you fell?"

I slowly shook my head. *Had I?*

"You hit your head, Henrietta. Maybe you don't remember everything," she added with a kind smile.

"Maybe," I said, trying to push out the cobwebs from my brain. "Anyway, how are things with you and Wally?"

Mary's face turned a light shade of pink. "Ooh, everything's good. Mostly. He went to Minneapolis last week for a few days. Not sure what it was for, and he won't discuss it."

"Are you still worried that he's having medical issues?"

"Yes, although he seems fine. He never complains about his health. I guess he'll tell me when he's ready."

We were interrupted by an orderly who came through the door. He headed to my breakfast tray, clanged the cover over the plate, and picked it up. With a nod toward us, he left without a word. I turned my attention back to Mary and changed the subject. "I need you to do a favor for me if you would. It's important. I need you to find my knapsack and my duffel bag."

"Your knapsack and duffel from the field? They're in the lab."

"They are?"

She nodded. "Yes, they're under your worktable with your tent. Hans probably stuck them there. Do you want me to bring them to you?"

A sense of relief settled in my bones. "First, I need you to look inside them."

"Okay . . ."

"I found something. Fossil eggshells. And what I think is a small skeleton. They're encased in two blocks of sandstone."

Mary radiated a big smile. "Wow, how exciting!"

"I wrapped them up. The eggshells are in my duffel and the rock containing the bones is in my knapsack. I hope they didn't get crushed. I want you to prepare them for me. Will you work on them? I don't trust anyone else."

"Of course! I'd be happy to."

"And Mary, if you don't mind, can you not tell the field crew about them?"

"Well, I hardly see them . . ."

"I know. But don't leave the specimens out where anyone can see them."

She pursed her lips. "Okay. But why not?"

I paused. "I have my reasons."

Her eyes narrowed. "Can I show them to Wally?"

"Of course. He's funding the excavation. But can you ask him to keep it under wraps? Until we know if the finds are significant?"

She reached out and squeezed my hand. "Don't worry about a thing. I'll get to work on them this afternoon."

"Thanks, Mary."

"I'll swing by later in the week and let you know how it's going. And I'll bring your clothes and knapsack."

Now all I could do was wait. Something that I did not excel at in the least.

The casserole dish wafted a heavenly scent as Janine entered my living room. Diane and Michael followed in her wake, like mice after the Pied Piper. My recuperation at home had begun. I closed the front door and joined the queue headed toward my kitchen.

"I brought you a hot dish," Janine said over her shoulder as she set the pan down on my counter.

I inhaled deeply. "Oh, thank you, Janine. That smells wonderful. Frank will be thrilled to get some decent food. And so will I." I settled heavily onto a kitchen chair.

The children stood quietly, each hugging a small doll. Diane stared at the cast on my arm. I pointed to it with my good hand. "I broke my arm," I told her. "That's why it's in a cast."

Janine cleared her throat and addressed her children. "What do we say to Mrs. Bailey?" she asked.

Diane and Michael looked up at me with solemn eyes. Together they recited, "We hope you feel better soon, Mrs. Bailey."

I tilted my head and smiled. "Well, thank you. I'm feeling better already. I see you've each brought a toy with you."

Michael lifted his arm. "This is G.I. Joe," he said. "Diane brought Barbie."

I pretended to consider the dolls. "Hmm. G.I. Joe is a good-looking guy. Maybe he should ask Barbie out on a date."

Michael crinkled his nose. "Ew, that's gross," he said.

Diane shook her head. "Barbie has a boyfriend. His name is Ken."

"Oh, I didn't realize that," I said. I turned to Janine. "Would you like some coffee? Frank made some before he left."

"Sure, if it's already made. Let me get it." She shooed her children out of the kitchen. "Why don't you two go play in the living room."

Janine puttered around my kitchen, locating the cups and filling them from our Melitta coffee maker. She set mine in front of me and poured one for herself.

"So how are you healing?" she asked as she slid into a chair opposite me.

I sipped my coffee and let the brew warm my throat. "I can't believe how tired I am. I didn't realize recovering from surgery would take this much energy. I can hardly do anything before I fall asleep. And my incision is so ugly," I said, waving my hand across my belly.

She nodded. "I know exactly what you mean. I had a C-section with the twins. Combine what you're feeling with having to feed two babies all day and night. I was a mess."

"I cannot imagine," I said. "You must have been exhausted."

"Exhausted barely covers it. Hormonal. Miserable. Crying. It's amazing John still speaks to me after all the names I called him."

She grinned slightly at the memory. "But time passes and you heal. Although I don't plan on doing it again. Ever. Two is enough."

I glanced into the living room. Diane and Michael sat on the couch, heads together. Low murmurs of Barbie's and G.I. Joe's conversations reached the kitchen.

"Can I ask you . . ." I hesitated, drawing in my breath.

Janine lifted her eyes from her cup. "Ask me what?"

"Maybe this is too personal, but did you always want to be a mother?"

Janine thought for a minute, leaned back in the chair, and emitted a small sigh. "To be honest, not really. I grew up on a ranch in the eastern part of the state. What I wanted was to get as far away from there as possible. I thought maybe I'd go to nursing school, but I met John in high school, and one thing led to another."

"So you got married?"

She shrugged. "Yeah." She lifted her cup and took another gulp of coffee. "I don't regret it, of course," she added, belatedly. Then she hesitated and studied me. "Why?"

A lump formed in my throat. I swallowed it down as my eyes rimmed with tears. "I don't know what the future holds for me," I said. "But after this accident, I don't think children are in the cards."

Janine reached over and grabbed my hand. "I'm sorry to hear that, Henrietta, honestly. Are you sure?"

"The probability is low, according to the doctor."

"Well, doctors don't know everything, do they? When I took Michael to the emergency room, the doctor told me that he might lose his leg. Can you believe that? Look at him now. I wouldn't put all my trust in one doctor if I were you."

How selfish did I feel, complaining to Janine after she had dealt with that news about Michael's leg? I squeezed her hand.

She continued. "And if you can't have a child, you can always adopt, you know. It's all just a matter of figuring out what you want."

Ah, just that.

CHAPTER 27

We never did talk about it, Frank and I, about the possibility of never having children. At least not that summer. As my wounded abdomen healed, a wall built quietly around the subject. Each hesitation was a brick. Each platitude, a slap of mortar. I knew Frank was concerned about me. But a closeness that had been there before had gone missing, fallen between the cracks. I grieved alone without understanding the full reason for my grief. And attempted to keep up the facade.

In addition to the awkwardness, Frank was tired of hearing me rave about the buried *T. rex* skull.

"So they hid a *T. rex* from you. There's nothing you can do about it. I told you they didn't want to share intellectual property with you. And frankly, why should they? They discovered the *rex* last summer and you weren't even there."

I glared at him. "Then why keep it a secret from me? They could have just told me that I wouldn't be included in any publications."

Frank laughed sharply. "Yeah, right. And how would that have gone over with you? After you had spent your whole summer digging it out?"

He had a point.

"Not well, I admit."

"There you go."

Weeks passed as I recuperated at home. My fatigue still overwhelmed me. I read and napped. My left arm, itchy and useless, healed inside the cumbersome cast. I wondered what was happening in the field but had no way of knowing. A single bright spot each day was when Mary called on the telephone with an update on her progress.

"Hello, Henrietta. I'm reporting in. How are you feeling?" she asked one day.

"Weak," I said. "How's the specimen?"

"I finished extracting the eggshell fragments. There are thirteen tiny pieces. I've put them together as best I can, and they make up about two-thirds of an egg. The egg is about two centimeters end to end, so pretty small."

"That's great. If the animal turns out to be a reptile, it might have laid the egg. It would be about the right size. Or it could have been a bird that nested underground."

"Yes, or if it's a mammal, it might have carried the egg down into the tunnel," she said. "I've started on the skeleton, but only part of the skull's uncovered so far."

"The important parts are the teeth. The teeth will tell us if it's a mammal or a reptile."

"All right, I'll keep working on the skull, then."

"Keep me posted. Thanks, Mary."

I did not tell her about the tyrannosaur. In the back of my mind, I wondered if Wally Whitehurst knew about its discovery. Was he complicit in shutting me out? I did not want to think that. He had hired me as part of the field crew after all. But I knew I was gullible, and I had certainly paid the price for that in the past.

Labor Day was approaching. It seemed like a nothing holiday, at least to me. If one were not working, then why celebrate a holiday for workers? The only milestone that mattered to me right now was getting this scratchy, miserable cast off my arm, which would not happen for another week.

Frank tossed some extra clothes into his duffel bag. His wildcat well had reached its total depth, and he was heading out for the final logging run. The oil industry did not care about something as irrelevant as a federal holiday. The rigs worked seven days a week.

"Do you have enough groceries?" he asked.

"Yes, I'll be fine. It's nice of Warhawk's geologist to pick you up."

"Yeah. I didn't want to leave you here without a car," he said. "In case of an emergency only, right? You still aren't supposed to be driving."

"When do you think you'll be back?"

"A couple of days," he said. "Wish me luck!"

"You don't need luck," I said. "The mud logger detected a show of oil, right? I'm sure the well will be a discovery."

A horn honked in our driveway.

Frank leaned over and gave me a perfunctory kiss. "I hope so," he said. "So I can shove it in George's face. The son of a bitch."

He hefted his duffel bag and headed out. The door slammed behind him, and I watched out the front window as he climbed into a truck and sped away.

Behind me, the phone jangled. I crossed to the telephone table and plopped down on the couch. "Hello?"

"Henrietta, it's Mary. I've cleaned off part of it."

I knew immediately what she meant. "And?"

"The skull and upper vertebrae are uncovered. You'll have to look at it."

My heart did a little flip. "Really? Are any of the teeth exposed?"

"Yes. They're small."

"Are they differentiated?"

Mary paused. "What do you mean?"

"Are there different types of teeth? Are there molars and premolars?"

"Oh. I don't think so. They all look the same to me. And sharp. But I'm no expert."

"All right. I'll try to drive in this weekend and look at them."

"Are you supposed to be driving?" Mary asked.

"Sure," I said, crossing my fingers. It was a straight shot into Dickerson. *How hard could it be?*

"Listen, Henrietta. The field crew is around. They've been coming and going all week. Just a heads-up, in case you don't want to run into them."

"Oh yeah? Thanks," I said, leaning back on the cushion. "They must be finished for the season."

"Evidently. They rented a flatbed truck, with ramps and chains, and took it to the site."

"I guess they decided to bring the bones in from the field after all," I said.

Of course, I knew they had always intended to do so, the lying pack of weasels.

"Yes. Wally says they've spent a lot of the museum's budget on transporting them. I hope they're worth it. Anyway, I've been keeping your skeleton out of sight. Your tent is still folded under your worktable. The skeleton is wrapped up in a box on the floor, hidden behind your tent."

"Great. I'll check it out as soon as I can."

Time to be sneaky. It would not be a *T. rex*, but perhaps my discovery would be an important find as well. And I certainly would not be sharing credit for it with anyone except Mary.

CHAPTER 28

Avoiding the empty museum lot, I parked behind the warehouse next door, stepping out of the car into the nighttime shadows. I felt like a female James Bond on a clandestine assignment. I had even worn a black shirt, black slacks, and my quietest Keds. My key slid into the lock and the museum's side door yielded. I crept down the hallway to the prep lab as my heartbeat rumbled in the quiet. Sneaking inside, I peered across at my station and made my way in the semidarkness, step by step, toward my desk lamp. The observation window overlooked the slumbering bony shadows in the dinosaur hall. The closest dinosaur, the *Stegosaurus*, seemed to glower at me as if in disapproval of my illicit errand.

My right hand rested on my still tender, swollen abdomen. My left arm with the cast extended out in front of me like a shield. I reached the lamp and pulled its chain. The incandescence spread across my worktable. Swiveling my chair out of the way, I slowly knelt and reached under the desk. My hand encountered the piled canvas of my pup tent, where it had been tossed. Stretching behind it, my fingertips felt the edge of a crate and the scratchy burlap fabric enshrouding the skeleton inside. I inhaled a quick bite of excitement. What did the skull look like, now that Mary had prepared it with her meticulous hands?

I pulled out the box with my right arm and maneuvered it to the lab table. It was heavy, and my abdominal muscles screamed in protest. Setting the fossil down on the table and holding my breath, I gently peeled away the burlap strips on the top. There it was, finally, in front of me. My mouth dropped open in wonder as I noted the pristine quality of the skull's preservation. Although the preparation was incomplete, I could still see that the bones were articulated, the upper vertebrae in place. I was not a dinosaur expert, but I knew some basic morphology. Larger than my fist, the skull had bladelike teeth, with the back teeth showing serrations, like tiny steak knives.

This was no mammal. The animal was a reptile. And a carnivore. The circular eye socket stared blankly up at me, indicating that the animal had a wide-eyed view. The size of the nasal cavity evidenced that the animal used its sense of smell to detect prey. Most importantly for identification, in front of the eye socket was a larger opening in the skull. This characteristic was also found in tyrannosaurs. The size of the opening told me not only that this was a dinosaur but that it was a theropod. This dinosaur had been a raptor. A small one. But a meat-eating predator nonetheless.

Was this a new species? The features reminded me of the bird-like *Compsognathus*, but I thought the skull's shape was different. One thing was apparent: I needed a dinosaur expert to examine the skeleton. And I was not going to trust Theo Small. I inhaled a deep breath as the solution popped into my head. I would call my dad. He would know someone at the Smithsonian. An expert he trusted. Somehow, I would get this fossil to Washington. I pondered whether to go ahead and take it with me. I could ship it to the Smithsonian and have someone there complete the preparation. I hated to take it away from Mary, but . . .

Just then I heard the squeak of the museum's outer door. Someone was entering the building. Subdued voices carried across, blue-shifting toward the lab. In a flash, I reached up and extinguished the lamp. I stuffed the burlap back into the box and pulled it into my chest. Crouching, I scurried across the lab to the coat cabinet. Fortunately, the cabinet door was ajar and I elbowed it open, climbed inside, and set the skeleton at my feet. Pulling the door shut, I closed myself inside just as the lab door squeaked open.

"I swear I saw a light on in here." It was Hans's voice.

Theo's voice answered. "I told you to stop smoking so much weed. That stuff will make you paranoid. Now you're making me nervous."

A switch clicked in the lab, and a fringe of light glowed around the edges of the cabinet door. I hunkered inside, not daring to breathe. A loud thud echoed, like a heavy box dropped to the floor.

"Look, I'll just be glad when this whole thing is over," Hans said.

"Me too. But don't blow the circuit now. The sale will go fine."

"You've met the buyer? He's got the money?"

Sale? Buyer? What the heck . . . ?

Theo replied, "Yes, I've met with the buyer and given him all the assurances. Everything's all set. So don't be a downer. Besides, you don't have as much to lose as I do if we're caught."

"Oh, yeah? Okay, for you to say, 'Dr. Important.'" I heard a foot kick something on the floor. "Anyway, this mess of bone shards will give the lab flunkies something to work on. And keep Whitehurst off our backs."

I wondered what Hans would think if he knew one of the "lab flunkies" was listening. The seam of light at the cabinet door's edge shadowed as the lab door opened again.

Theo called over. "Are all the crates at the barn?"

Rob's voice answered. "Yeah, all there."

Hearing Rob's voice, I felt a ping of sadness. He had been the one to rush me to the hospital. I thought he was a decent guy. Apparently not.

I listened in silence, the cabinet walls pressing in on me, coffin-like. The air grew stale. With my recovery incomplete, exhaustion washed over me like a tsunami. So much for being James Bond.

Rob's voice came again. "What's our timing on the sale?"

"The buyer's coming next Sunday night for the skull. Midnight. At the barn," Theo said.

"A quarter of a million, right?" Hans asked.

"Oh yeah, it's a lotta bread. He's depositing half of the money in my account on Saturday. We get the other half after he gets the skull."

"Just make sure we get our cut when it's all over," Hans said.

There was more shuffling before the light extinguished. I heard the outer door slam.

Shimmering with rage, I waited for what seemed like eons before daring to lunge back out into the lab. I leaned against a worktable and gulped some fresh air. The men had vanished as if I had dreamed the whole conversation. But I had not. The crew had brought in the bones of a *T. rex*. And they intended to sell them. Or at least sell the skull. Removing me from the dig had nothing to do with sharing intellectual property. It was greed, pure and simple.

Anger burned behind my eyes. I returned to the cabinet and retrieved my skeleton. Carrying it back toward its original hiding place, I stubbed my toe on the new box of bones on the floor, which made me even madder. I silently swore like Frank would have in my mind.

Fossils were treasures, not commodities. They were meant to be studied scientifically. And enjoyed by the public in museums. The *T. rex* bones belonged to the Dickerson History Museum. It was illegal to sell fossils from a dig on BLM land.

My gut churned with acid, and not from my wound. It was up to me to stop this sale. Who could I get to help me? Was Wally Whitehurst part of this scheme? Hans's disparaging remark about Wally aside, I still did not know the answer to that question.

Shaking with fatigue, I set my skeleton back in its hiding place behind my tent. It would have to wait. I would go through the proper channels to get it to the Smithsonian. Suddenly it seemed important to follow all the rules.

I had a more pressing mission now.

The dry September air filtered through our few screened windows, the sashes thrown open, turning the living room into a moisture-less vacuum. The distant clattering of a tractor infiltrated as a monotonous backdrop in my ears. Exhausted after my exertions the previous day, I barely made it to the phone when it rang.

"Hello?"

Mary's voice vibrated down the line. "Henrietta, I wanted to tell you our news!" she said without preamble.

"News?" I asked as I lowered myself onto the couch.

Mary offered a radiant laugh. "Yes! Wally and I are getting married! He proposed last night."

I tried to muster some excitement through my fatigue. "Congratulations—that's wonderful. Although my aunt always says that I should say 'best wishes' to a bride and not 'congratulations.'" Pulling my legs onto the couch, I settled back against the cushion.

"We've decided to get married as soon as we can. Wally said he has some business to attend to first, but we're leaving next Monday."

A hard knot began to form in my stomach. *What kind of business did Wally have?* I wondered.

"Oh? Next Monday? One week from today?" I asked.

She plowed on, oblivious. "We'll drive to Denver and get married at the courthouse there, with his son and daughter-in-law as our witnesses. Then we're driving to Minneapolis to meet his daughter and her family. It will be a rolling honeymoon."

Her joy hummed through the handset.

I replied, glad she could not see my face as I clenched my jaw. "How lovely. I guess you won't be back to the lab for a while?"

"A couple of weeks, yes. By the way, did you get to the museum to see the skeleton over the weekend?"

I paused for a moment. "No. I wasn't feeling up to driving," I lied. "I'll try to get there soon."

"Of course. I hope you'll be feeling better by the time we return."

I cleared my throat. "I'm sure I will. We'll have to go out to lunch and celebrate when you get back."

"That would be wonderful. I look forward to it."

As I set the receiver in its cradle, I stared blindly out the open window. Any consideration of asking Mr. Whitehurst for help was now out of the question. The timing seemed too suspicious to my mind. What if he was involved after all?

The minute the clock hit five I dialed my parents' phone number. If I could rely on anyone for advice, it would be my dad. After four muffled rings, my mother answered.

"Hello, Ballantine residence."

"Hello, Mother, it's Henrietta. I'm calling to speak to Dad."

My mother replied, "Honestly, dear, you could at least talk to me for a few minutes first. How are you feeling?"

"Much better thanks. I'm healing well and getting up and around."

"Well, don't overdo it. You need to rest," she said. "Your dad isn't here. Didn't he tell you? He's in Williamsburg, helping Dr. Miller with a new whale discovery."

I took a deep breath. "Oh, I don't think he mentioned it. When will he be back?"

"Next week sometime."

After chatting with my mom for a few more minutes I hung up the phone. Exhaustion tugged at my shoulders.

Who could I call to help me now?

With my arm itching beneath the cast until I wanted to scream and my brain worrying about my quandary, I could not sleep that night. Frank was still in Montana. My dad was out of reach. I thrashed like a zombie in my empty bed. A third-quarter moon lit the room through the half-closed blinds as I deliberated about what to do next. Finally, a solution began to formulate in my mind. I sat up in the dark, my covers knotted around me like an osprey nest.

I could contact the newspaper and get a reporter interested in covering a big scoop—the discovery of a *T. rex* skeleton by the museum's field crew. The reporter would bring a photographer, and they could do a front page spread in the *Dickerson Press*, with photographic evidence. I would arrange for all of us to meet the field crew at the storage barn. After all, I knew the day and time they would all be there. I would stop the sale of the *T. rex* and scare off the buyer. At three o'clock in the morning, it seemed like a brilliant plan.

If Frank had been home, I would have run this solution by him. Instead, I needed to act alone. And quickly. Who did I know at the *Dickerson Press*? Faye Monroe, of course! I would call her in the morning.

I rooted around in the kitchen junk drawer and found the old invitation to the Monroe's Christmas party, crammed in with the batteries, pens, paper clips, and assorted detritus. I brushed off the cardstock and read their telephone number at the bottom, next to the RSVP.

Settling in next to the phone, I dialed, the rotary clacking along with my nerves at each number.

"Monroe residence," a female voice intoned.

"Hello, Faye?"

"Who should I say is calling?"

"Henrietta Bailey."

"One moment, please." The phone clattered down in my ear. I heard "Thank you, Betty," and then "Hello, Henrietta?"

Suddenly I was tongue-tied. "Yes . . ." *Why* had I called Faye? She jumped into the silence. "How are you? I should have called for an update after your accident but didn't want to bother you."

I found my voice. "I'm doing better. I'll get the cast off my arm this week. Thank you so much for the flowers you sent to the hospital."

"Our pleasure. I'm glad you're on the mend. What can I do for you?"

"You're still with the *Dickerson Press*, aren't you?"

Her distinctive tinkling laugh fluttered in my ear. "Oh yes, I'll be with them until they put me under the sod. I'm writing a column now about the Labor Day picnic at the Catholic church. Why? Did you have something in mind?"

"I know you write the social column, but do you ever write about other events? Like something having to do with the museum?"

"Oh sure, sometimes. We're a pretty small outfit."

"Well, I have a situation, and I need your help . . ."

And then I told her everything. About the crew finding the dinosaur skeleton, hiding it from me, and bringing the bones to the storage barn. About the overheard conversation and the illegal selling of the skull. She listened without interruption.

Then I offered my plan.

"I know they're meeting the buyer this coming Sunday night at midnight. You could meet me at the barn early and bring a photographer with you. Once the field crew gets there, we can appear and I'll act like I'm giving a big press announcement. The photographer should bring some bright lights and take lots of photos. You can interrogate them and write an article for the front page. The buyer will be scared away. And there will be a public record of the *T. rex* discovery. What do you think?"

She paused so long I thought she had set the phone down.

"I think it's a great idea," she said finally. "Let me run it by my editor first."

"Okay. The bones in the warehouse will just look like chunks of rock covered in plaster. We'll have to catch the crew in the act and hear them talking about the *T. rex* to prove what's inside. It will be somewhat clandestine. So be sure to keep everything quiet, on the down-low for now. If the buyer or the crew finds out, then the whole thing might be scrapped."

"Oh, honey, don't worry," she said in her fairy voice. "I'll be as quiet as the grave."

CHAPTER 29

The front door slammed, and Frank's heavy footsteps trod into the living room exfoliating dirt. His clothes rumpled, a two-day shadow of a beard framed his face. He dropped his duffel bag on the floor and stood with his hands on his hips, a thoughtful look on his face.

"My well came in," he announced.

I looked up from behind the newspaper, with the headline THURGOOD MARSHALL SWORN IN AS SUPREME COURT JUSTICE, and scrunched my face at Frank. "It came in where?" I asked.

He replied, "That means it hit pay. Fifty feet of oil. Tested at five hundred barrels per day." His voice had a flat quality, like pond water, although I was sure something was swimming underneath. Exhaustion shadowed his eyes.

"That's fantastic! Isn't it? Your idea was correct."

He frowned and sank heavily into the empty upholstered chair across from me with a sigh. "Yeah, it was correct. And what royalty will I get for it? Zip."

"But Monroe Petroleum will still get their royalty, right? Isn't George excited?"

He burst out a bitter laugh. "I called George from the rig to let him know. Do you know what his reaction was? He was furious. He just about came through the receiver at me. Said I didn't push the play enough. Didn't try to convince him to drill it. Now he's lost money and according to him, it's my fault that he farmed it out."

"Well, that's not fair. I know you tried to get him to drill it."

"You know what? Life's not fair. Not in this case."

I got up from the couch and walked behind him, leaning over and hugging his neck with my good arm.

"Oh, honey, I know all about life not being fair," I said, kissing the side of his face.

He sighed and leaned his head back against me. "And how has life been unfair to *you* this week?"

"Well, let me tell you what's happened . . ." I said. And then, instead of letting him relax, I launched into an explanation of the events of the past few days. Since I could not see his face, it did not dawn on me that this was a mistake. His shoulders tensed, which should have clued me in, but I kept going with my story. Once I was finished, he turned around to stare at me. Then he erupted like Krakatoa.

"What the hell, Henrietta! Are you out of your mind? You drove into town—never mind that you aren't supposed to be driving—and hid in a coat closet? While Theo, Hans, and Rob hatched an illegal plot to sell the *T. rex*?"

I nodded, numbly, as I stared at the thunder in his face.

"And then, instead of telling Wally, or calling the police, you call my *boss's wife*? And try to get the newspaper involved? And now my boss probably knows too? My boss, who is furious at me?"

His face turned an unusual purplish hue.

He continued. "And what do you expect to do? Ride in on a white horse and save the day?"

"Only metaphorically," I said, pursing my lips. "And I told you, I'm not sure Wally isn't involved. And I have no proof to offer the police."

Frank ran his hands through his hair. "Am I supposed to go with you on Sunday night? To this debacle? You know it could be dangerous, right? There's a lot of money involved here. Do you think everyone's just going to walk away once you prance in?"

My lower lip began to quiver. "Well, I guess I didn't think that part all the way through. Faye will be there. And a photographer. And yes, I thought you'd want to go with me. As my backup."

His response was unprintable, but I did not think it would be approved by the Presbyterian church. Or any denomination, for that matter.

Two hours later Frank drove me to Dickerson General Hospital. "Although I don't know why," he grumbled, "since you can obviously drive yourself." It was a long, deeply silent trip.

I perched on a metal examining table as a doctor freed my pale, mended arm from my cast. Hallelujah. I wanted to kiss him.

Afterward, I exited into the waiting room. Frank sat with his arms crossed, his mouth a grimace. I was definitely *not* in the mood to kiss *him*.

At least one thing had been mended that day.

I waited all week for a call back from Faye. I imagined her like Lois Lane, blonde flip bouncing up and down as she convinced her editor, spinning the story of our covert plot to expose the thieves. In my mind's eye, I could see the editor, a Perry White character, nodding in agreement, hollering for the best photographer, who rushes into his office. The photographer, Jimmy Olsen-esque, plotting the lighting and camera positions to get the best shots. We were the team who would stop the sale of this North Dakota treasure. Perhaps I had seen too many *Superman* television episodes.

In actuality, I heard nothing from her. Silent as the grave, indeed.

By Friday afternoon, leaving behind my fantasies of the *Daily Planet*, I dialed her number. After several rings, she answered.

"Faye? It's Henrietta Bailey. I'm wondering what your editor said. Are we all set for Sunday night?"

Her laugh seemed rather shrill. "Oh, yes, we're all set."

"You'll be at the barn?" I asked. "With a photographer?"

"You betcha."

"At midnight?"

"Wouldn't miss it."

"Frank and I will meet you in the parking lot."

"That sounds like a plan, honey."

"See you—"

The dial tone rang like a hollow promise in my ear.

CHAPTER 30

Frank and I parked our car behind the abandoned farmhouse on the road to the storage barn. I glanced at my watch as the headlights extinguished. The inky blackness of the night settled around us like a black sheep's fleece.

Frank gripped the steering wheel. "You know this is crazy, right?" he growled.

"It will be fine," I said for the hundredth time. "Faye will meet us out front with a photographer."

"And then we'll ambush Theo, Hans, and Rob, not to mention the buyer? And they'll throw their arms in the air, recognize the error of their ways, and repent?"

"Yes. Exactly," I said.

"Woman, you are some kind of crazy. And I'm crazy for not talking you out of this."

"Come on," I said. "We've got to hike down this road. It's forty minutes until showtime."

Frank reached underneath his seat and pulled out a long leather sheath.

"Whoa. What's that?" I asked, pulling back from him.

"My fishing knife," he said. "Just in case." He slid the sheathed knife, blade first, inside the sleeve of his flannel shirt.

We exited the car and gingerly closed the doors. I was dressed in my clandestine black, accessorized with a deeply frowning husband. I could hardly see but did not want to use a flashlight. My heart began to steadily increase in speed as we walked along the dirt edge of the gravel road, single file, Frank in the lead. Ahead, the outline of the barn came into view. A lone lightbulb shone outside the front door, drawing a cotillion of fluttering moths. No wonder the spiders made webs there. The haze illuminated Theo's pickup truck, parked diagonally.

"Faye isn't here yet," I whispered ahead to Frank.

I could make out the outline of his head, nodding in the dark. "This way," he said, his voice low, leading me into the shadows at the side of the building.

"Now what?"

"We wait, Nancy Drew, what else?"

We lingered in the darkness, food for pests. Mosquitos swarmed around my face and nipped at my neck. Spiders lurked in cinder-block crevasses. Just as my anxious heart began to settle, I heard a vehicle approaching, its tires crunching over the gravel. A large pickup truck pulled into view. It swung around in front of the barn and backed against the bay door.

Frank grabbed me and pulled me against him, his mouth to my ear. "That's George's truck."

My heart lifted. "Can you see who's driving? It must be Faye. Is a photographer with her?"

We peeked around the corner as the driver's door opened. The inside of the truck cab illuminated. A hunting rifle hung in a rack along the back window. Only one person was inside the truck. But it was not Faye.

It was George Monroe.

George stepped out of the truck, closed the door with a click, and looked around the lot. We pulled our heads back around the corner of the building. The sound of his boots diminished as the front door opened with a rusty creak. Voices filtered outside, and then the door slammed shut. Silence.

I looked up at Frank and whispered, "Do you think George came instead of Faye? To expose the sale?"

Frank looked down at me, his eyes piercing through the darkness. "Only one way to find out. Let's try to listen at the door."

We left our hiding place and scurried across the lot, scooting around George's truck, and headed toward the front door. Exposed by the lightbulb, I tried to hunch over to minimize my profile. My palms began to sweat and my heart beat a tom-tom in my chest. A light glowed from inside, but no sounds escaped.

Then a loud screeching noise vibrated in the air as the giant bay door began to heave open. Frank grabbed me and we hurtled behind Theo's pickup truck and hunkered by the far front tire. Hans and Rob appeared, pulling on a chain to raise the door.

George and Theo stepped out of the garage. "Back your truck about halfway inside. We've got the skull on the forklift," Theo said.

Rob ducked back inside the garage, and I heard the chug and screech of a forklift.

I peeked over the hood. George slid into his truck. The engine flared and the truck reversed into the garage, the cab sticking out into the lot. I used the noise to cover my voice.

"Frank, do you think George is the *buyer*?" I whispered.

"It would appear so," Frank said through gritted teeth.

I looked at him. "That can't be, can it?"

"Of course it can. Think about it. Who else around here has the money to buy a *T. rex* skull?"

I thought back to the Christmas party at the Monroe's house. The shelves of Indian artifacts. The decorative geodes. The opulent food and decor. A *rex* skull would be a crowning glory in their living room.

How stupid had I been to call Faye. Thinking she would help me. I had played right into their hands.

The truck ignition purred off. George climbed out, shut the driver's door, and opened the back one. He reached inside and grabbed his hunting rifle off the rack. Turning, he gripped the rifle in both hands, his back to the truck. Instead of walking into the garage, he stood and surveyed the area.

I hardly recognized his face. Gone was Frank's jovial boss from the Christmas party. His backbone upright, his eyes were hard slits in his craggy face.

"Henrietta Bailey, are you out there?" he hollered. "Show yourself! And you too, Frank."

I looked at Frank, my eyes widening like saucers.

Hans and Theo froze, paralyzed, their eyes scanning the lot.

"No one's here but us . . ." Theo began, his voice shaking.

"Oh, shut up. They're out there," snarled George. "Come on out. Frank! Henrietta! Now!"

Frank and I looked at each other. As one, we rose from behind Theo's truck.

"Come on out from behind there," George called with a wave of his rifle. "And put your arms in the air."

We did as we were told, walking forward with our arms raised. My heart whipping in my chest, my lungs hyperventilating, I stared with venom from George to Hans to Theo. Rage rolled through me.

"So, you're buying a *T. rex*," I hollered at George. "Found on BLM land. Which is illegal, you know. It belongs to the museum."

George took a few steps toward us. "These bones were found on my land," he said, a sneer on his face.

"No they weren't. I was there. I saw them in the ground."

"Prove it," he snarled.

I glared over at Hans and Theo. "And you're selling it to him?"

"What the hell are you doing here?" Hans hissed, his voice slithering toward me.

"I'm standing up for the museum. Which is more than I can say for you, mister 'lab manager.' And what about *you*?" I roared toward Theo. "A paleontology professor! Are you selling your soul here?"

Theo stared from the rifle to me, panic on his face. He opened his mouth to answer but was cut short.

"Shut up!" George yelled at me with another wave of his gun. "You two heroes, in the garage. Go!" He turned and yelled into the garage. "Put that chunk of rock in my truck! Now!"

Frank and I walked forward. The whir of the forklift surged, and George's truck sank and rebounded, letting out a shrill creak as the full weight of the rock-encapsulated skull landed in the truck bed.

"Keep walking," George said, gesturing with his gun for us to enter the garage. I walked inside, with Frank behind me. Plaster dust hung in the air, stinging my eyes. George walked in behind us. "By the way, Frank, I'm sure it's obvious, but you're fired."

"Fine by me, asshole," Frank growled at him.

Tears came to my eyes, but I blinked them away. Ahead of me, Rob turned off the forklift and emerged from behind its steering wheel. He stared at us, an unreadable expression on his face.

"Tie these two up and shut the place down," George ordered Rob. "Hurry up."

Rob looked around and grabbed a ball of twine hanging on a peg. He unwound it while he approached us. Stepping behind me, he pulled my hands around my back and bound my wrists. "Sorry about this," he said in a low voice.

"I'll bet you are," I said, spitting out the words. The twine bit into my wrists, making me wince.

Frank put his hands behind his back, allowing Rob to tie his wrists together.

"Now, sit down," George said to us. "Tie their feet together too," he ordered Rob.

We sat on the hard dirt floor. Rob wound twine around our ankles, pulling it tightly.

"Are you going to just leave us here, tied up?" I asked George.

"Consider the alternative," he said, his face cracking a sadistic grin.

Finished with binding us, Rob crossed to the front of the bay and flicked a series of switches, extinguishing the lights. "I'll need to strap down the pallet in the back of your truck," he said to George.

"All right," George growled. He disappeared outside. A minute later his truck pulled out of the garage. Rob gave us a last look, then walked over to the chain and released it, lowering the door.

He ducked outside just before the door slammed into place with echoing finality.

Huddled on the floor in the darkness, tears threatened to spill from my eyes.

"Frank," I sniffled. "I'm so sorry."

"It's all right, Henrietta. We're okay."

I leaned against him. "Yeah, but we're tied up and stuck in here. Who knows when someone will come to the barn next? It could be months."

Frank grunted in the dark. "Oh, we won't be here that long," he said, sliding his fishing knife down his arm inside his sleeve. "I've got the handle of my knife in my palm. See if you can grab it and cut me loose. Without slitting my wrists."

I wiggled around so my hands touched his and felt the wooden handle of the knife. Frank held the leather sheath with his fingertips and I pulled the blade free. I tried to manipulate the blade to cut the twine on his wrists.

"Ow, damn it, you stabbed me," Frank whispered.

"Sorry," I whispered back.

A few minutes later, I sawed through his bindings. "Rob did a good job on these knots," Frank groused, tossing away the bits of twine. "The son of a bitch." He grabbed the knife and cut his feet loose. Then he freed me.

We stood in the blackout and listened. The purr of the truck engine and voices reached us through the garage door.

"I don't think we should leave through that door," I whispered.

"No. Is there another way out? Besides the front door?"

"There's a side door on the far wall of the barn," I said.

"Do you think you can find it in the dark?"

"Maybe," I said, rubbing my wrists. "Follow me."

"All right, let's go."

The barn's interior was as dark as a cave. I hurried across as quickly as I could, my hands out in front of me like a spelunker without a headlamp. My blood coursed in my veins. "I can't see my fingers in front of my face," I whispered.

My left foot struck something hard and I stumbled. Frank caught me. "Careful."

"If we ever get out of here, I'm going to strangle someone," I said, gritting my teeth.

"Not if I get to them first."

A tiny strand of light appeared up ahead. A filthy porthole in the far side door allowed a smidgen of moonlight inside. "This way," I whispered.

We reached the side door and slowly cracked it open. A waning gibbous moon rose in the east, providing minimal light. We slipped out into the night.

"Now what?" I asked. My heart raced faster and my palms began to sweat.

"Let's see what they're doing," Frank said, his voice low and steady.

We crept along to the front corner, placing our feet soundlessly in the dirt. We peered around the far edge of the barn. Theo's truck was still parked in the shadows, not far from our position.

Frank signaled me with his hand to follow. We squatted down and raced on tiptoe to a stack of pallets near the truck. Hunkering behind them, we observed the activity across the lot. Hans and Rob worked in the back of George's truck, passing a strap to each other, securing the pallet to the bed. George and Theo stood by the hood, facing each other, speaking in low tones. George still gripped his rifle in one hand.

Hans leaped out of the truck bed. Rob gave the strap a few final tugs, jumped off the back of the truck, and slammed the tailgate closed.

"All set," he said.

George opened the driver's door and tossed in his rifle. He slid into the seat and slammed the door shut. Leaning out the open side window, he called out, "Remember, I never met you. And you never met me."

"Right," Theo managed, his voice thready. He backed away and joined Hans as they turned to walk across the lot toward their truck. And toward us.

Then, several things happened simultaneously. Rob walked forward to George's open window. Reaching one hand behind his back, he pulled out a handgun tucked under his shirt. He pointed it at George through the window.

"Federal agent," he declared, in a surprisingly official voice. "Don't touch your gun. Get out of the truck. You're under arrest."

Theo and Hans turned to look at Rob, their faces stunned. They looked at each other and, with eyes widened in fear, broke into a sprint in our direction, heading for their truck.

George, eyes glaring, nostrils flaring, shoved his truck door open with violent force. The door slammed into Rob, knocking him off balance. Rob fell backward, his gun firing up into the sky with an explosive bang. He landed on his back, sprawling in the gravel. The gun dropped to the ground beside him.

On a reflex, I sprung up and dashed across the lot. "What the hell are you doing?" Frank yelled at my back as I ran. I ignored him, passed Theo and Hans, and rushed toward Rob.

At the same time, George slammed the door shut and floored the accelerator. Rob rolled out of the way as the truck fishtailed out of the parking area, spewing gravel. It roared down the road.

I reached Rob and knelt beside him. He clutched his shoulder in the dirt.

"Get the gun," he moaned.

I grabbed the gun off the ground and, without thought, aimed with both hands at the fleeing truck. I pulled the trigger.

The gun fired with an ear-piercing blast. By some miracle, the bullet found one of George's tires.

The tire exploded like Vesuvius. Rubber tephra flew through the air. The truck veered side to side, screeching on its metal rim. It plummeted off the road and came to rest, listing sideways in a ditch.

I stared in astonishment, my heart thudding in my chest.

I turned in time to see Theo and Hans reach their truck. Frank was in motion. He grabbed Hans by his shirt collar and forced him to his knees. Hans looked up at Frank and sneered. "Ah, the husband, come to save the day?"

Instead of replying, Frank leaned over and punched him solidly in the jaw, dropping him to the ground.

"Don't get up," Frank told him.

Theo stood at his tailgate and stared, white-faced and shaking. Frank walked over to him and pushed him up against the truck. I saw the glint of the fish knife as Frank pulled it out of his back pocket.

Sirens began to wail, and red lights pulsed like beacons down the road.

Rob and I looked at each other. "Give me the gun, Henrietta," he said, pulling himself off the ground.

"What?"

"The gun," he said. "Give it back to me."

I looked down at my shaking hands, pointed the gun's barrel downward, and handed it to him.

The sirens grew louder. The lights materialized as the roof-mounted flashers of police cars. One car was emblazoned with a large star and SHERIFF on the side. It pulled next to George's crippled truck.

Rob studied my face. "Are you all right?" he asked.

"Yes, how about you?"

He nodded as he wrapped his right hand around his left shoulder. "I'm okay, but I think I dislocated my shoulder when the door hit me."

"Federal agent, huh?"

"BLM law-enforcement officer," he said, grimacing in pain. "This takedown sure did not go according to plan."

We looked down the road at George's truck, teetering sideways on two tires. Two police officers were maneuvering George out of the cab. There seemed to be an abundance of swearing happening. On both sides.

"Good thing you tied down the *rex*," I said to Rob.

He barked a laugh, then groaned as he gripped his shoulder. "Yeah, good thing."

We turned and walked back toward Frank. Hans sat crumpled on the ground, nursing his aching jaw. He glared at us as we approached. Theo leaned with both hands against his truck, looking like he was about to faint.

"Good hit, babe," I said to Frank.

"I aim to please," he said, a grin stretching across his face. "It helps to have a lot of pent-up rage."

CHAPTER 31

Over our fifteen months in North Dakota, we had purchased one major item. I sighed inwardly as I watched our television set retreating from our house in a truck bed. Frank sold our set to Warhawk's geologist, and it was on its way to a new home. Our free collection of Esso juice glasses rested in a kitchen cabinet, left for future renters, a testament to our long commute. Other than that, we accumulated no new furniture, no knickknacks, no housewares. We packed up our lives in the same suitcases and boxes with which we arrived. From an outside glance, our arrival and departure looked like bookends. Not that anyone was looking,

"I left an astronomy textbook and a geology textbook for Diane and Michael," I said. "I know they're way too young for them, but maybe they can read them when they're older."

Frank shoved one last box into the back seat of the station wagon. "Good idea. No room for them anyway."

"I've got a stack of books to give back to Kima," I said. "Can we stop on the way out?"

"Who's Kima?" Frank asked distractedly.

"The Indian woman who runs the used bookstore. I want to say goodbye to her."

"Oh, sure. But it's Sunday. Do you think it's open?"

"I don't think she has any particular schedule."

Slamming our car doors, we pulled out of the driveway. The tires churned up clouds of dust that wafted inside the car's back windows. One last souvenir of North Dakota dirt.

We crossed the empty highway and pulled in front of the bookstore.

"The sign's not out. I don't think she's here," I said.

Frank peered through the windshield. "It looks like there's a light on inside."

"Okay, I'll check." I reached down and scooped up the pile of books by my feet.

The door yielded but the bell failed to jingle as I pushed inside. The stacks appeared more dilapidated than usual, and the moldering smell of old books made my nose crinkle. A dusty film covered the cash register. The baskets by the back door were missing. An aged man puffed on a cigarette in the corner chair. He seemed vaguely familiar.

"Hello. I didn't think you were open. The sign's not out front," I said.

This got no response from him.

"I came to return these books," I persisted, holding the stack up in front of me.

"Just leave 'em on the desk there," he said, his voice like sandpaper. He pointed with his cigarette. "I don't pay for returned books, ya know."

"That's all right." I glanced around. "I'm leaving town and wanted to say goodbye to Kima. Is she here?"

He blew out a smoke ring that surrounded his mustache and stared at me through the haze. "Who?"

"Kima. The Indian woman. She works here?"

He coughed a series of wet barks and looked with rheumy eyes. "Nobody here but me."

"Can you give her a message?"

"No idea who yer talking 'bout," he said. He went into a further spasm of coughing as I set the books down.

"Are you okay?" I asked.

He nodded and waved me away through his coughing fit. I turned and left the shop.

Popping back into the station wagon, I mulled over what the man meant. Did he mean that Kima was not there *today*? Or *ever*?

Frank backed the car out and headed for the highway. "On to the museum?" he asked.

I snapped out of my musings. "Yes. Time to pick up my treasure."

A brown carpet of grasses now spread across the high prairie, the once green tassels dried from the baking sun of early autumn. The exit for Dickerson loomed ahead. We pulled off along the numbered streets, twisting and turning, wordlessly taking in our last views of the town. We passed Monroe Petroleum, which looked locked up and buttoned down. All the window shades were drawn. On the far edge of town, the museum appeared deserted, the lot empty.

I used my key and we entered the side door. We walked down the dim hallway, past the restrooms and water fountain, and I pushed open the paleo lab door. Reaching up, I flicked on the lights. A sense of melancholy settled over me as I viewed the workspace. I had endured the endless North Dakota winter days working here, chipping away at rock-encrusted bones. Even with all the heartrending experiences of the past weeks, I would miss this place. My Garden of Eden within the frozen, snow-covered landscape.

Frank and I crossed to my workbench. An open wooden crate awaited us. On the lid beside it, the label read DR. HENRY BALLANTINE, U.S. NATIONAL MUSEUM. My dad had agreed to serve as the official recipient of the fossil skeleton. Experts at the Smithsonian were ready to examine my find.

A noise sounded, and I turned to find the engaged couple, Wally Whitehurst and Mary Tremaine, coming through the door.

"Mr. Whitehurst! Mary!" I said. "It's so nice of you to come and see us off."

Mary smiled broadly. "We wouldn't miss saying goodbye. Plus I wanted to see your expression when I show you what I've uncovered in the past few weeks."

"I'm sorry you had to postpone your wedding," I said.

"It's not your fault. When the sheriff called us and told us what happened at the barn, we knew we needed to stay," Mary said.

Wally walked forward using his crutches. "I wanted to tell you how sorry I am about the way the dig ended," he said. "And to thank you for trying to stop the sale of the *T. rex*. Without you two, I'm not sure the sheriff would have made an arrest."

"Oh, I'm sure he would have. With Rob's help, of course."

Wally replied, "Well, we're grateful. I understand that George Monroe is protesting his innocence and threatening litigation, so the whole thing may drag on for a while."

"Sorry we'll miss hearing about *that*," I said, sarcasm in my voice.

The four of us circled the worktable and stared down at my dinosaur skeleton nested in the crate.

"You weren't kidding, Mary. You've done a lot more work on the skeleton in the past three weeks," I said.

She pointed toward the fossil. "Yes. There are two skulls, aren't there?"

I reached down and traced my finger around the dinosaur's skull. A sense of reverence settled around me. "You can see this is a theropod skull, here," I said. "The skull openings and teeth are characteristic. And look here." I pointed to a newly exposed forearm. "See these three long claws at the end of the digits? They're small but deadly. This was definitely a raptor."

"I can't believe how intricate the skeleton is," Frank said, seeing it for the first time. "At least the part that's uncovered so far. The bones look to be in great shape." He pointed farther along the skeleton. "That does look like a second skull, doesn't it?"

I lowered my head and examined the block closely. "You know, I think it is." I beamed at the group. "There's another animal in there. I guess once the fossil gets to the Smithsonian and the rest is uncovered, we'll see what else might be in there."

"Be sure to let us know what you've found. We're both interested to hear what the experts say," Wally said.

"I will. I promise to keep you both apprised. After all, the fossil belongs to this museum. My dad will make sure it's returned."

Mary pointed at the bottom of the box. "The eggshell pieces are all wrapped in that burlap bundle there."

"Thanks, Mary, for all your hard work. And for packing up everything so carefully. We'll take good care of the crate on the way to Washington. And who knows . . . maybe you and I can publish an article about the fossil in a scientific journal someday. Wouldn't it be fantastic if we've uncovered a new species?"

Mary's smile spread across her face. "I would be honored to do that with you."

I dug into my pocket and pulled out my museum key. "Here, Mr. Whitehurst. I don't think I'll be needing this anymore," I said.

"It might be time to get the locks changed anyway, considering all that's happened," he said, reaching for it. "And Henrietta, do you think you could stop calling me Mr. Whitehurst and call me Wally instead? You're making me feel old."

I laughed. "Of course."

"Time to go," Frank said.

He lifted the fossil-containing block out of the crate, and Mary covered it with cotton batting and wrapped burlap strips around it until it was packed like a chrysalis. They fitted it back inside the box, and Frank hammered the wooden lid in place at the corners. With the crate cradled in both arms, Frank headed out of the lab, followed by Wally. Mary waited for me at the doorway. I stood for a last moment, gazed across the paleo lab, and said a mental goodbye. Then with a click to extinguish the overhead lights, I turned toward Mary and let the door shut behind us.

"I'll miss you, Henrietta," she said. "The lab won't be the same without you."

"I'll miss you too, Mary. But it looks like everything worked out for you and Wally. By the way, did you ever find out why he made those trips? I know you were worried about his health."

She laughed. "Yes, it wasn't that at all. He was visiting his children, telling them about me, and letting them know he wanted to remarry. He wanted to get their permission first. Isn't that sweet?"

What if they'd said no? I did not ask. We walked to the parking lot, and I gave her a final hug.

The crate now nestled safely between two suitcases in the back of our station wagon, Frank slammed the tailgate closed, like the grand finale at the end of a fireworks show. We said our goodbyes, and Wally and Mary waved to us as we pulled out of the lot for the last time.

"Onward," Frank said to me. "Looking forward to spending some time at home?"

I nodded. "I'm looking forward to visiting our parents. And finding out about this fossil. Or I should say *fossils*, plural."

"Then on to New Orleans?" he asked.

"Yes. Good thing you made inquiries when you did. I'm ready for our next adventure," I said, giving him my biggest smile.

We merged onto the highway and headed east into the North Dakota sunshine. Neither of us bothered to look in the rearview mirror.

EPILOGUE

PRESENT DAY

Rolling my suitcase behind me, I exited the Dickerson Regional Airport and took in the North Dakota view. Inhaling deeply, I looked skyward. The aquamarine expanse loomed overhead, as familiar to me now as it had been fifty years ago, extending in all directions across the flat terrain of the High Plains. Lofty thunder-heads gathered in the west, portending afternoon showers. I wanted to get to my motel before then.

Keys in hand, I crossed the airport parking lot to locate my rental car, wheeling my suitcase behind me. My numbered spot held a gray Camry. I slid my suitcase into the back and settled into the driver's seat. The odor of stale cigarettes, mixing with the new car scent, made my nose crinkle. I dug my cell phone out of my purse, turned it off airplane mode, and sent a text.

Arrived in ND. Flights okay.

The car engine ignited and I gripped the steering wheel with my age-spotted hands. Nothing I could do about those blemishes—such was the fate of a geologist with years of working outdoors in the field. As I adjusted the side mirrors, my phone chimed.

A thumbs-up, with a heart emoji.

He always had been a man of few words. Putting the car in gear, I headed away from the airport.

Noting new developments on both sides of the highway, I exited and headed for Dickerson's First Street. Fracking had transformed both the petroleum industry and the North Dakota landscape since I'd last visited. The ability to fracture nonpermeable source rock, in this case the Bakken Shale, had caused a mass influx of oil field workers to the state. Releasing the copious reserves of oil held within the tiny pore spaces required skilled laborers—roughnecks, roustabouts, drillers, mud loggers—and they had come. From Texas, Oklahoma, and Louisiana, arriving in droves, often bringing their families. Trailer parks had sprung up overnight, then subdivisions, to accommodate the influx. And the supporting infrastructure followed to feed, clothe, and entertain the immigrants. I was anxious to see the changes, one in particular.

My head spun trying to recall the town's landmarks as I navigated with my phone. Better to use Google Maps than my memory. I recognized the building that had housed Monroe Petroleum. It was now a bank, the company long ago absorbed in an industry merger. A shiny elementary school, family dental clinic, and triplex movie theater, all new to me, appeared as I drove along. I turned by the brick public library, which had been a one-room clapboard shack, and passed a community college, the modern academic buildings occupying what had once been a cow pasture. So many changes.

Heading east to what had been the outskirts of town, the Dickerson History Museum appeared in front of me, my heart's home during that fateful year. I laughed to myself, my heart swelling, as I noted the changes. The once flat roof had been raised, the front entrance now glassed with two-story windows catching the midday light. A new wing sprouted majestically, giving the building an eagle-like appearance. I pulled into the parking area, now paved, and let my mind wander. Here was the place where everything changed for me. Where my naivete had been shaken and my marriage tested.

I decided to wait until tomorrow to step inside. I was being honored at a dedication ceremony. A bit of history resolving itself. It was about time.

My room at the Holiday Inn was a cookie-cutter version of every other motel room across the country. I piled up the pillows and draped myself along the king-size bed. Why was flying so tiring? I reached up and unbraided my hair, running my fingers through the strands to separate them. I still wore my hair long, although it now shone in a pure white hue. Maybe one day I'd cut it. Or maybe not.

I pulled my phone from my purse and dialed. It rang twice.

"Hello, beautiful," Frank answered.

"Hello, handsome," I replied.

"How's Dickerson?" he asked.

"Different," I said. "The museum has a whole new wing. I'll send you some photos. How's the symposium going?"

"Good so far. I'm so sorry it fell on the same weekend as your award ceremony. I wish I could be there."

"Me too. But since you're the keynote speaker, it wouldn't have worked for you to skip out," I said. "How have the sessions been?"

"Very interesting. Lots of new ideas on heat transfer, plate motion, and mineral recrystallization at depth," Frank replied.

Frank was still working, long after most of his colleagues had retired. Always a "big-picture geologist," his hypotheses concerning East Coast tectonics had both ardent followers and vocal detractors.

"Well, I'm sure your ideas are the most controversial."

He laughed out loud. "You're right about that. Good thing I have thick skin."

The next morning, I took a deep breath as I pulled open the glass doors and stepped into the two-story, sun-swept atrium of the museum. The dark, dingy entrance with the guest book was a thing of the past. Light poured in through the new high windows,

illuminating the exhibits. The dinosaur skeletons had been recon-
figured on modern platforms, ringing the space. Tarps covered two
exhibits waiting to be unveiled—one gigantic and one small. Rows of
folding chairs faced forward toward a podium in front of the larger
shroud. Of course, I knew what was underneath both. They were
why I was here.

I took a few steps as my eyes took in the view. A young man—
most looked young to me now—swept up to me, hand extended.

"Dr. Ballantine! Welcome!" he said. "I'm Andrew Peterson, the
museum curator."

"Hello. Please call me Henrietta. And thank you for inviting me,"
I said, shaking his hand.

"We're very excited that you're here. The ceremony will start in
about an hour."

"Yes, I thought I'd have a look around first if that's all right."

"Of course! Let me know if you need anything. Please seat yourself right there in the front row once the ceremony begins." He indicated the lines of chairs.

I thanked him and moved farther inside. The new wing sprouting to the left was labeled WALTER WHITEHURST MEMORIAL HALL.
I walked across the atrium, briefly admiring the dinosaur skeletons,
and entered the new gallery. A plaque on the wall stated, "This hall
is dedicated to the memory of Mr. Walter Whitehurst, museum
director, chemist, and wildlife photographer." On the walls, Wally's
wildlife photographs hung in new frames. I had forgotten how beautiful they were. Lingering in front of the photo of the prairie dogs,
I remembered when Frank and I saw the noisy rodents when we'd
hiked the badlands. I swallowed the sudden lump in my throat and
continued down the hall.

The updated signage reflected current scientific thought.
PALEOECOLOGY OF GREAT PLAINS FAUNA read one. CLIMATE
CHANGE ON THE PRAIRIE read another. I recognized some of the
artifacts from long ago—the old grain cradle and the cast-iron stove.
A reproduction of a sod house had been built for children to play

in, with prairie clothing in a trunk for them to try on. An interactive video game along one wall allowed visitors to pack their own Conestoga wagon. I wondered if it was possible for people today to imagine crossing the prairie, fearful of drought, weather, starvation, and Indian attack.

The alarm on my phone buzzed, reminding me to head back to the atrium. Visitors were taking their seats. A docent handed a printed page to me as I approached. I inched my way to the front row, sat at the end, and glanced at the sheet in my hands. "Prehistoric Predators Unleashed: Unveiling a Fierce Giant and a Stealthy Hunter." The museum director approached the podium. Behind him, the larger exhibit remained hidden with tarps and ropes.

"Good afternoon and welcome. Thank you for coming. I'm Andrew Peterson, one of the curators here at the Dickerson History Museum. I'd like to welcome you today to the unveiling of our two new dinosaur exhibits. The expedition to retrieve these skeletons from the badlands was funded by this museum, with the foresight of none other than Mr. Walter Whitehurst, former museum director, to whom our new wing is dedicated. The fossils revealed today were discovered and retrieved from the badlands in the late 1960s. I direct your attention first to your left, to our exhibit titled 'A Stealthy Hunter.'"

The heads of the crowd swiveled toward the smaller tarp.

He continued. "The skeleton I'm about to unveil is unique in several ways. First, it is a skeleton of the smallest theropod dinosaur discovered in the world to date. The size of a large chicken, this dinosaur was a stealthy hunter, feeding on small mammals with serrated teeth and vicious claws. The skeleton was found within an ancient burrow complex, much like one dug by prairie dogs today. The burrows had been infilled with sand during a flood, preserving the bones inside. Second, this fossil is unique because, inside its stomach cavity, the skeleton of a small mammal was found perfectly preserved. The size of a modern-day chipmunk, it tells us what the dinosaur ate for its last meal. And third, a dinosaur egg was discovered in a side chamber of the burrow.

"Therefore, it is clear that this theropod dinosaur moved into the mammal's home, built a nest for its eggs, and then ate the mammal for breakfast. This is what's known as habitat usurpation, which can be inferred here by the discovery of this fossil thief and her prey."

He motioned to two members of his staff, who walked over and slid the tarp off a glassed display case.

"From the North Dakota badlands and the Hell Creek Formation, I give you the theropod dinosaur *Kleptodon fossilis*, with the mammal skeleton in its gut and its reconstructed egg."

Appreciative applause rippled around me like a rising tide. I felt a smile spread across my face. There was my discovery, delicately prepared by Mary, and on loan until recently to the Smithsonian archives. The skeleton was displayed at an angle in the case, lying on a tilted sandstone substrate. From my seat, I could see the artist's rendition of the animal painted on the back of the display. The painting depicted the dinosaur perched inside the burrow, with a mouthful of glistening pointy teeth. An extended forearm ended in tapering claws. In the image, a shrew-like creature quivered in a corner, about to become prey.

"Be sure to take a closer look at *Kleptodon* after the ceremony," the director said, "to truly appreciate this remarkable discovery."

He turned his attention to the canvas behind him and gestured toward it with his arm. "I'll move on to the 'Fierce Giant.' As you may know, the next specimen was under litigation for many years. Eight years ago, the skeleton was shipped to the Field Museum in Chicago for preparation, paid for by a grant from the George and Faye Monroe Charitable Foundation. It has now been returned to us here."

He moved away from the podium, signaling again to his two staffers. They stepped to one side of the giant tarp, unhooked ropes from pulleys, and slowly lowered the covering to the ground.

A collective gasp went up from the crowd. I gazed in amazement, my chest swelling in awe. A magnificent *Tyrannosaurus* skeleton emerged from within the drape. It was even bigger than I had imagined. Standing on a wide pedestal, it posed with its massive head tilted upward, jaws wide, as if roaring toward the sky. The sun shone off the bones, highlighting them from behind so they glowed with a warm umber radiance.

The crowd applauded exuberantly as cell phone cameras clicked. The director stepped back behind the podium.

"I give you our *Tyrannosaurus rex*. He has been named Theo, after Dr. Theo Small of Dakota State University, who first discovered the bones. We don't know if our *T. rex* is male or female, but for simplicity, we'll use male pronouns. Theo is one of the largest and most complete *rex* skeletons ever found. He measures thirty-five feet long and stands ten feet tall at the hip. His skeleton is eighty percent complete. His skull alone weighs over five hundred pounds."

I stared up at the knife-edged teeth in the gaping jaws of the skull. Could it have been fifty years since I last saw those teeth? In the middle of a stormy night, encased in matrix, under a flapping tarp?

"Two members of the field crew who discovered *Kleptodon* and unearthed Theo are here today. I'd like to ask Dr. Henrietta Ballantine and BLM park ranger Robert Harkness to come forward."

At the end of the row of chairs, a man stood. He turned and grinned at me as I rose from my folding chair. Rob Harkness, after all these years. A little thicker around the middle, with a lot less hair, he sent me a brief wave as we approached the podium from opposite ends. I gingerly climbed the steps, my knees not being as stable as they once were. We flanked the podium and smiled at one another.

The director pulled out two plaques from a shelf within the podium and handed one to each of us. "With many thanks for your hours of fieldwork, the museum appreciates your dedication in bringing these fossils home," he said. He shook our hands, and we headed back to our seats as the crowd once again applauded.

I looked down at the plaque. Did I deserve this recognition? Yes, for discovering the *Kleptodon* skeleton. But I had spent only a few weeks digging at the *T. rex* site. After that, I had been shuffled aside. Without Rob's undercover work, the *rex* might have disappeared into a private collection. Frank and I had helped to prevent that from happening. Who knows where the skeleton would be if we hadn't?

The ceremony concluded, and the visitors swarmed forward to get closer views of the *T. rex* and of *Kleptodon* and the mammal.

I walked over to the new exhibit case and stared down at my fossil find. The preservation of both the dinosaur and the mammal was exquisite. The bones of the small mammal stood out against the sandstone, encased beneath the predator's rib cage. The egg had been meticulously pieced together so that the cracks were barely visible.

"Well, Henrietta Ballantine. It's been a long time."

I looked up. "Rob Harkness! Yes, it has. Good to see you."

"You too. So this is what you found when you left us each day, hiking out by yourself across the badlands?"

"Yep, this is it. Although as I remember it, I was pushed away by the three of you."

"As you know now, that was Theo and Hans's idea." He nodded toward *Kleptodon*. "That's a nice discovery. A two for one, shall we say?"

"I was just lucky. I found the bones when I hammered one of the burrows and it broke off. It happened the morning I fell off the cliff. The skeleton was wrapped up in my knapsack."

"Oh man, I'll never forget that day. I was scared to death driving you to the hospital."

"I don't have much memory of anything after I fell," I said. "I don't even remember calling for help."

Rob's eyes turned thoughtful. "You know, it was so strange. I remember it like it was yesterday. Theo tried to contact you when we started to pack up, but you didn't answer. Then the walkie-talkie started squawking, you know, and there was this loud whooshing noise. I mean really loud, like the wind in a tornado. That's when I drove overland and found you on the ground."

I felt something inside me shift as if a long-forgotten puzzle piece slid into place. "I'm not sure I ever thanked you, Rob, for driving me to the hospital. So if I didn't, I'm saying it now—thank you." We moved out of the way to let others see the display and meandered over toward the *T. rex.*

"It's something, isn't it?" Rob said as we stared up at the *rex.*

"It sure is. I can't believe they named it after Theo, though." Rob laughed. "Yeah. What a lark. He came out as a hero. At least to some."

"Whatever happened? I never heard all the ins and outs," I said.

"The skeleton was tied up in litigation for years. It was locked up in a government warehouse. George claimed he'd donated the money to Theo for 'paleontology research.' In the end, we couldn't prove that he was trying to buy the skeleton. Of course, he lost the money. Since he claimed he'd given it for research, it had to be used for that. Theo never benefited personally from any of it—at least he couldn't spend the money on himself."

"But it probably funded his fieldwork for years."

"Oh yeah, it probably did."

"What happened to Hans?" I asked.

"Wally fired him, and I heard he moved to Fargo not long after he was arrested. He wasn't supposed to leave the state until after the case went to trial, but it stretched out so long, and then it was settled out of court. I don't know what happened to him after that."

"And the Monroes?"

"They both passed. They never had any children, so Faye set up the charitable foundation before she died. I think she regretted the whole episode. Word got around, you know, that George tried to buy a dinosaur found on BLM land. I think there were some cold shoulders after that, even with all their money."

"At least the museum dedicated the new wing to Wally and not to the Monroes," I said. "What about you? Did you stay a federal officer?"

"Sure did. For over thirty years. I worked out of the BLM office in Belle Fourche, down in South Dakota. Still live there. My daughter's in the area, and my grandkids. One of my granddaughters is a wildlife biologist. She studies large mammals like bison, can you believe that?"

I laughed. "Following in your footsteps."

"What about you, Henrietta? Where are you living now?" he asked.

I replied, "Virginia. Frank and I live on a small farm about an hour outside Washington, DC. I'm retired now, but Frank's still working at the USGS."

Rob looked thoughtful. "The last I heard, the two of you were headed for New Orleans. Did you work in the oil patch down there?"

I stood for a moment and looked up at the *Tyrannosaurus*. Its wide eye socket offered me a death stare, and its daggerlike teeth glinted in the sunlight. I shivered slightly. So much had happened since I had first seen that skull, embedded in the Hell Creek Formation in the badlands.

"Well, Rob, that's a long story. A very long story indeed."

POSTSCRIPT

Vertebrate Paleontology Bulletin (1971), vol. 54.

New Reptilian and Mammalian Taxa from Hell Creek
Formation, Cretaceous, Southwestern North Dakota by
Henrietta Ballantine and Mary Tremaine Whitehurst

Abstract: Two new Cretaceous (Maastrichtian) taxa are named from southwestern North Dakota. *Kleptodon fossilis*, a new species of Cretaceous dinosaur, has been discovered within a large-diameter burrow and chamber complex in floodplain deposits of the Hell Creek Formation. One of the smallest theropods yet discovered, the taxon is represented by a complete skeleton, forty-six centimeters (eighteen inches) in length, with characteristic bladelike serrated teeth, clawed forearms, and hind legs. Analysis of its skull shows that *Kleptodon* had a high bite force quotient for its size. Fossil eggshell fragments found within a side chamber of the same burrow indicate the dinosaur used the chamber for nesting. Carnivory is confirmed for *Kleptodon*, as its stomach cavity contains a complete mammal skeleton. Here named *Eovora dakota*, an extinct member of the Eutheria, the specimen is the size of a modern-day prairie dog pup. *Eovora* is distinguished by its classic dental pattern of incisors, premolars, and molars. The complexity of the burrow-chamber complex, described herein, is analogous to that of modern mammal burrows. Therefore, it is proposed here that *Eovora dakota* dug the burrows, but *Kleptodon fossilis* usurped them, laying eggs within a side chamber and consuming *Eovora* pups. The etymology for the proposed taxa names comes from the Greek: *Eovora dakota* meaning "Early Dakota Prey" and *Kleptodon fossilis* meaning "Fossil Thief."

AUTHOR'S NOTES

Thank you for joining me for Henrietta Ballantine's latest adventure. In 1998, I was fortunate to participate in a dinosaur dig in North Dakota with the Marmarth Research Foundation. Much of my description of the badlands was taken from this trip. As noted in the last chapter of the novel, North Dakota has undergone an economic boom with the practice of fracking, a technology that did not exist in the 1960s when Frank worked in the petroleum industry. I tried to be true to the geological techniques used at that time. As stated, few specimens of *Tyrannosaurus rex* had been discovered by the 1960s. Nowadays, famous *T. rex* skeletons grace major museum exhibits. Sue, from South Dakota, stands in the Field Museum in Chicago. Peck's *rex* and the Nation's *rex*, both from Montana, occupy halls at the Museum of the Rockies and the Smithsonian, respectively. With the discovery of Sue in the 1990s, the subject of fossil ownership became national news, as the landowner, the federal government, and the Black Hills Institute of Geological Research battled over that *T. rex* skeleton. So there is precedent for litigation to occur over a *T. rex*. Fortunately, Sue did not disappear into someone's private collection.

Dinosaur taxonomy has also changed since the 1960s, with the acceptance of cladistics and the discoveries of feathered theropods and studies of birds. I characterized my dinosaurs as reptiles, per

Linnaean classification at that time. The species *Kleptodon fossilis* and *Eovora dakota* are entirely of my imagination.

Many thanks to my family, friends, and colleagues who shared their experiences with me and aided in the writing of this novel. As always, to my husband, Bob, who is my biggest encourager, geological adviser, and spitballer, thank you with my whole heart. I couldn't do it without you. Thank you to my children, Marie, Brett, and Anna, who have given me support and advice throughout my writing journey. Since I have never been to North Dakota in the winter, many thanks go to Ernie and Deanna Dvorak, who shared stories of life in North Dakota. Ernie grew up in a small town in North Dakota, and his input was invaluable to this story. (Shelterbelts? Who knew?) Thank you to John and Sue Zager for sharing their experiences of living in Wyoming and working in the oil fields. I am indebted to Derek Raisanen for sharing his master's research and knowledge about fossil mammal burrows. Thank you to my beta readers, Susan Bare, Ellen Bearden, Roxanne Chandler, James Lyon, Nancy Ochsenreiter, and Susan Barnes Whitehead, who provided invaluable feedback on this book. I appreciate all the support from my writing colleagues in our author's club, Lake Authors of the Wilderness. Thank you to my team at Bublish, the editors, the technical team, and the artists. They are responsible for my wonderful cover and chapter art and for evaluating, copyediting, and formatting the manuscript.

SHORT BIBLIOGRAPHY

Carson, Rachel. *Silent Spring.* New York: Houghton Mifflin, 1962.

Nerburn, Kent. *Neither Wolf Nor Dog: On Forgotten Roads with an Indian Elder.* Novato, CA: New World Library, 1996.

North Dakota Game and Fish Department, *Prairie Wildflowers and Grasses of North Dakota,* https://gf.nd.gov/sites/default/files/publications/prairie_wildflowers_grasses.pdf.

Raisanen, Derek C. W., and Stephen T. Hasiotis. "New Ichnotaxa of Vertebrate Burrows from the Salt Wash Member, Upper Jurassic Morrison Formation, South-eastern Utah (USA)." *Annales Societatis Geologorum Poloniae* 88 (2018): 181–202.

Safina, Carl. *A Sea In Flames: The Deepwater Horizon Blowout.* New York: Crown Publishing Group, 2011.

Spencer, Robert F., and Jesse D. Jennings, et. al. *The Native Americans: Ethnology and Backgrounds of the North American Indians.* New York: Harper and Row, 1965.

Utley, Robert M. *The Last Sovereigns: Sitting Bull and the Resistance of the Free Lakotas.* Lincoln, NE: Bison Books, 2020.

Van Enk, Glenn, R. H. Heintz, P. L. Crogen, and E. P. Lana. *Growth and Survival of Shelterbelts,* North Dakota Research Report No. 75. Fargo, ND: North Dakota State University, 1980.

Made in the USA
Middletown, DE
03 April 2024

52328010R00146